GOLD & Heartbreak

CELEBRATING CANADIAN HOCKEY
from ANTWERP 1920 to TORINO 2006

Fenn Publishing Company Ltd.

GOLD & HEARTBREAK
Celebrating Canadian Hockey from Antwerp 1920 to Torino 2006

A Fenn Publishing Book / First Published in 2006

Designed by First Image
Fenn Publishing Company Ltd.
Bolton, Ontario, Canada
Printed in Canada

Acknowledgements

The author would like to acknowledge the tremendous and ongoing support of publisher Jordan Fenn. Additional thanks go to everyone at the IIHF for their support, namely Rene Fasel, Jan-Ake Edvinsson, Dave Fitzpatrick, Hannes Ederer, Kimmo Leinonen, Szymon Szemberg, Jenny Wiedeke, Thomas Freyer, Konstantin Komissarov, Rob Van Rijswijk, Federico Saviozzi, Gion Veraguth, Martin Zoellner, Darren Boyko, Eslie Dall'Oglio, Luzia Baldauf, Simone Micheletti, Peggy Arnold, Johanna May, Darryl Easson, Sofia Chatzis, Anna Eskola, Stephanie Kallai, and Andy Ecker. A special thanks to the great photographers Juka Rautio and Jani Rajamaki. To the incredibly helpful group at the Hockey Hall of Fame---Phil Pritchard, Craig Campbell, Darren Boyko (again), Peter Jagla, Miragh Addis, Danielle Siciliano, Izak Westgate, Ron Ellis, Mike Gouglas, Anthony Fusco, Kevin Shea, and Marilyn Robbins. Also to the talented and enthusiastic team at First Image design of Michael Gray and Rob Scanlan. To my agent Dean Cooke and his associates Samantha North (miss ya already) and Suzanne Brandreth. To those always near at hand, notably mom, Liz, Ian, Zachary, Emily, and Mary Jane.

GOLD& Heartbreak

CELEBRATING CANADIAN HOCKEY
from ANTWERP 1920 to TORINO 2006

Andrew Podnieks

Fenn Publishing Company Ltd.

Contents

It took some 18 years of professional hockey, but Joe Sakic has finally been named captain of Canada's most important hockey team. From the time he turned pro with the Quebec Nordiques in 1988 to the present day, there is virtually nothing this great centreman hasn't accomplished. In his final year of junior with Swift Current, after being drafted 15th overall by Quebec, Sakic led the WHL in points and was named the player of the year for all Canada.

After an excellent NHL rookie season in '88-'89 with the Nordiques, Sakic exploded for 102 points in his second year and 109 points the year after. In all, he has eclipsed 100 points five times during his NHL career, twice scoring more than 50 goals as well.

Sakic was named Quebec's team captain in 1992 and four years later, the team's first in Colorado as the Avalanche, he took the Nordiques to the first Stanley Cup in franchise history. He led the playoffs with 34 points, won the Conn Smythe Trophy, and lifted the Cup high after a four-game sweep of Florida in the finals. Among his 34 points were 18 goals, an NHL record, and two of those were overtime winners. Five years later, Sakic again led the Avalanche to the Cup, and again he led the playoffs in scoring. The 2001 finals was a hard-fought seven-game series against the New Jersey Devils.

Internationally, Sakic has answered the call for his country on several occasions, almost all of them successful. As a teen, he played at the World Junior Championship in 1988, winning gold. In 1991, he won a silver medal at the senior World Championship, and in 1994 he was part of the gold-medal team at the Worlds, the first gold for Canada since 1961.

Sakic also played at the 1996 World Cup and 1998 Olympics, the latter an abbreviated appearance because of a knee injury. His crowning glory came four years ago in Salt Lake City where he was a key member of Canada's first Olympic gold in half a century. Yet, at every turn of his international career, someone other than Sakic was team captain. His international appearance in Torino, at age 36, marks his first games with the "C" over his Team Canada heart.

Team Canada coach Melody Davidson had no reason to tamper with success. Cassie Campbell remains at the height of her powers, and as the woman who led Canada to Olympic gold four years ago in Salt Lake City, there was no reason not to name her captain again for Torino.

Campbell has done everything imaginable with her hockey career. She has been with the Women's National Team for 12 years during which time she has won six gold medals (1994, 1997, 1999, 2000, 2001, 2004) at the World Championship and one silver (2005). She has an Olympic silver medal from Nagano in 1998 to go with her 2002 gold.

In addition to her international career with Team Canada, Campbell has been among the most successful club players in modern women's hockey in Canada. She played four years of university hockey in Guelph (1992-96), and since 1999 has been a fixture in the NWHL, first with the Beatrice Aeros and for the last four years with the Calgary Oval X-Treme, winners of the WWHL Cup in 2004-05.

Throughout her career, Campbell has been a model spokesperson and promoter of the women's game, making public appearances, signing autographs, and commentating for TSN.

Canada 16 / Italy 0

February 11 • Palasport • 8:30 p.m.

It wasn't a baseball score; it wasn't a football score. But, it sure wasn't a hockey score, either. Physically overpowering, ruthlessly tenacious on the puck, meticulous in their positioning, superior skaters. Canada's women were so much the better team that much as their skill was to be admired, one couldn't but feel sorry for the Italian women whom they pummeled so thoroughly by a 16-0 score.

How quickly did the Canadians start the defence of their gold medal? Cassie Campbell had two partial breakaways, the team had five shots on goal, made three line changes, and scored once. That was the first 96 seconds of the game. Sixteen seconds later, the score was 2-0. Caroline Ouellette scored both goals. Despite all, the 8,399 faithful fans shouted, "Italia! Italia!" with championship fervour.

And so it went. Hayley Wickenheiser made it 3-0 at 4:04, and Ouellette completed her first-period hat trick at 6:53 on the power play to make it 4-0. Cheryl Pounder made it 5-0 playing four-on-four. By the midway point of the period, there was so much snow in front of plucky goalie Debora Montanari's crease it needed the Zamboni. By the end of the period, shots were an astounding 26-3.

"After the second goal," Montanaro said good-humouredly, "I asked my defenceman if every period is like this."

It was as easy as this looks. Hayley Wickenheiser scored twice, including this one thanks to a great pass from Cherie Piper.

GAME SUMMARY

First Period

1	Canada, Ouellette (*Hefford, MacLeod*)	1:36
2	Canada, Ouellette (*Hefford, Botterill*)	1:52
3	Canada, Wickenheiser (*Piper*)	4:04
4	Canada, Ouellette (*Botterill, Campbell*)	6:53
5	Canada, Pounder (*Kellar*)	11:34

penalties: de Rocco (Ita) 6:38, Angeloni (Ita) 10:42, Goyette (Can) 11:13, Goyette (Can) 13:56

Second Period

6	Canada, Vaillancourt (*Piper*)	0:25
7	Canada, MacLeod (*Campbell, Apps*)	2:32
8	Canada, Apps (*Piper, Wickenheiser*)	18:45
9	Canada, Wickenheiser (*Piper, Apps*)	19:56

penalties: Kellar (Can) 2:52, Bettarini (Ita) 10:46

Third Period

10	Canada, Apps (*Piper, Wickenheiser*)	1:35
11	Canada, Botterill (*Ouellette, MacLeod*)	7:31
12	Canada, Hefford (*Ouellette, Botterill*)	8:41
13	Canada, Pounder (*unassisted*)	9:42
14	Canada, Goyette (*Campbell, Sunohara*)	12:19
15	Canada, Apps (*Piper, Wickenheiser*)	16:15
16	Canada, Weatherston (*Agosta, Vaillancourt*)	17:37

penalties: Sostorics (Can) 3:37, Fiorese (Ita) 7:50, Bettarini (Ita) 5:34

In Goal

Canada	Kim St. Pierre
Italy	Debora Montanari (1st, 2nd)
	Luana Frasnelli (3rd)

Shots on Goal

Canada	26	21	19	**66**
Italy	3	2	0	**5**

Referee	Danyel Howard (USA)
Linesmen	Sanna Mattila (FIN)
	Ilse Robben (NED)
Attendance	8,399

Although Canada won the game in the first minute, coach Melody Davidson used the time to work on certain aspects of the team's game. "We wanted to work on things that would help us down the road," Jennifer Botterill admitted, "things like one-touch passing and a four-point attack so we're not just going straight to the net."

It worked. The Italian nightmare continued a mere 25 seconds into the second period when Sarah Vaillancourt scored on a delayed penalty. Two minutes later, Carla MacLeod scored on another delayed penalty, and the Canadians continued to storm the crease like the proverbial bumblebees. The partisan fans gave in to the relentless onslaught and amused themselves with song and doing the wave, and on ice Canada goalie Kim St. Pierre froze from inactivity. In all, she handled a mere five shots for the shutout (Canada had 66 shots).

Italian coach Markus Sparer mercifully inserted backup goalie Luana Frasnelli for the final 20 minutes, but she conceded a goal to Apps 1:35 after her debut. In all, she allowed seven goals in her one period of play. Despite the score, Montanari was Italy's best player. "I'm very tired but very happy," she said. "I play the game because I love hockey, but there are only 150 players in all of Italy. In Canada, there are so many."

Statistically, Cherie Piper led the way with six points (all assists). Right behind her were three teammates with five points: Gillian Apps and Ouellette had three goals each and Hayley Wickenheiser two goals.

The Canadians wore their Nike-swift sweaters, sporting a new black look with the 1920-style red maple leaf in the front. ♣

Canada peppered the Italians with 66 shots, the courageous Debora Montanari stopping 38 of the 47 shots she faced.

Finland 3 / Germany 0

February 11 • Esposizioni • 1:00 p.m.

"We'll definitely win," Finnish captain Sari Fisk said after the team's final practice before the start of the Olympics. And that's what happened the next afternoon as Finland cruised to a 3-0 win to open the women's tournament.

The trio of Mari Pehkonen, Karoliina Rantamaki, and Saara Tuominen was clearly Finland's most dominant line as it produced the team's first two goals. "I'm happy because we won, but our game needs to be better," said Rantamaki. "We were maybe a little nervous. This was our first game, and that was the biggest thing."

The Finns opened the scoring at 8:15 of the first when Heidi Pelttari took a point shot that deflected in off the skate of Pehkonen. The video goal judge ruled the puck was not kicked in and the goal stood.

Referee Arina Ustinova permitted incidental body contact, but the physically larger Germans ran into penalty trouble nonetheless. With Stephanie Fruhwart and Christina Oswald sitting in the penalty box, Pelttari gave Finland a 2-0 lead on the power play at 17:02, jabbing in a loose puck after Emma Laaksonen's point shot came off the end boards.

Marja Helena Palvila completed the scoring at 3:13 of the third when she intercepted a bad German pass through centre ice and walked in alone on goalie Stephanie Wartosch-Kuerten. The first women's game at the Palasport provided a result more surprising than expected as Sweden defeated Russia by a narrow 3-1 score.

Sweden 3 / Russia 1

February 11 • Palasport • 3:30 p.m.

The Swedes were the heavy favourites going into the game (in fact, the Russians finished dead last at the last World Women's Championship), but the Russians had the better scoring chances in the first 20 minutes.

"We were a little bit nervous in the first period," Swedish forward Maria Rooth admitted, "but then we just went out and played in the second. This was by far the best Russian team I've ever played against."

A holding-the-stick penalty early in the second put a halt to the Russians' enthusiasm as Nanna Jansson connected with a high wrist shot over the shoulder of Irina Gashennikova at 3:26 to give Sweden a 1-0 lead.

Less than two minutes later, Rooth made a nice pass to Katarina Timglas who one-timed the puck over that same blocker shoulder of Gashennikova. The Russians finally got on the board with just 39 seconds left in the second when Trefilova took a bad-angled shot that Martin deflected into the back of her defenceman. The puck trickled into the net to cut the Swedish led to 2-1.

Sweden got a lucky goal of its own early in the third when a point shot from Rooth bounced off a Russian defenceman in front and skittered past Gashennikova to make it 3-1.

"We didn't play well at all," Joa Elfsberg said, "but we won the game 3-1. They played a little better than we expected, but the score is the most important thing."

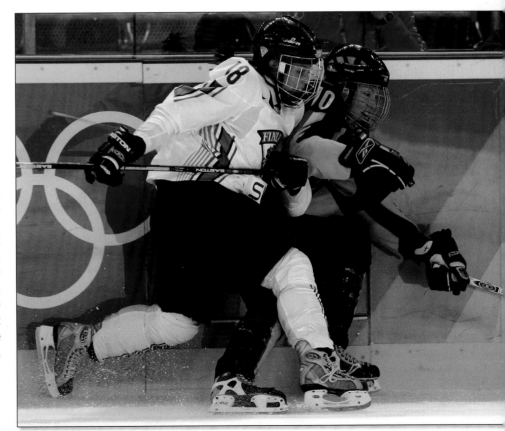

Finland's Satu Hoikkala checks Nikola Holmes of Germany during the first day of women's hockey at the 2006 Olympics.

USA 6 / Switzerland 0

February 11 • Esposizioni • 6:00 p.m.

The USA downed Switzerland 6-0 in the tournament opener for both teams. But for the outstanding work of Swiss goalie Patricia Elsmore-Sautter, who faced 56 shots, the score could have been double.

It was an intimidating introduction for the Swiss women who were playing their first Olympics. At 2:08 of the opening period, with the teams at four-on-four, Katie King took Jenny Potter's centering pass from behind the net and beat Elsmore-Sautter along the ice to put USA up 1-0.

The Swiss managed to keep the Americans at bay for most of the period with intense checking and solid positional play, even though most of the action was in their end. Elsmore-Sautter made two of her best saves late in the period, stopping USA captain Krissy Wendell twice.

Seemingly inspired by their goalie's performance, the Swiss began pressing around the American net. They were rewarded with overlapping five-on-three opportunities in the second, but it was USA that scored when Tricia Dunn Luoma blocked a point shot and made no mistake on the breakaway.

"That's a momentum-changer right there," Wendell said. "We had three guys in the box and they were going to be on the power play for a long time in a 1-0 game, so it was huge."

Midway through the second, Wendell converted a perfect Ruggiero pass to make it 3-0 and in the third Natalie Darwitz and Wendell broke the game open with goals. Jenny Potter rounded out the scoring with 1:10 left.

"I think our team played very well, with a lot of heart," said Swiss coach Rene Kammerer. "But the USA is a team built for the gold medal game, and we are number nine in the world."

Swiss goalie Patricia Elsmore-Sautter was the star of the day, keeping her team in the game until midway through the third period against a vastly superior USA team.

Flag-bearer Danielle Goyette

The first female hockey player to carry the flag at the opening ceremonies of an Olympics, Danielle Goyette completed a dream that she has been chasing all her life. One of eight children, she started skating at a young age and by age five she tried to play like her idol, Guy Lafleur. By her teens, she was playing organized women's hockey, and in 1991 she started her career with the women's National Team that has continued unchecked for 15 years. Now 40, Goyette has played in more World Championships than any other Canadian, man or woman (eight), winning seven gold medals.

On January 26, 2006, she was named Canada's flag bearer. "For the past 14 years," she explained at the press conference, "I've been wearing the maple leaf on my jersey, and it's always been an honour. But today is very special."

"I will carry the flag for all the athletes," she continued. "I know that all of your hands will be with mine as we walk in the stadium." Although Goyette was, in many ways, the ideal selection, she was not the first. Cross-country skier Beckie Scott, bobsledder Pierre Lueders, and speedskaters Cindy Klassen and Clara Hughes all declined the honour, fearing the duties of the flag-bearer and the opening ceremonies would prove wearying and affect their Olympic performances adversely.

Goyette's father passed away just days before the start of the 1998 Olympics in Nagano, Japan, but her inspired performance led her to a tournament-best eight goals. Four years later, she tied for the tournament lead with ten points at Salt Lake en route to Olympic gold.

Danielle Goyette carried the flag for Canada at the opening ceremonies and scored a goal the next night against Italy.

Canada 12 / Russia 0

February 12 • Esposizioni • 4:30 p.m.

It wasn't the Summit Series or the '87 Canada Cup, but it was Canada-Russia. Unfortunately, the women's rivalry between those two nations has not picked up where the men left off, and this afternoon at Esposizioni in Turin, Canada waltzed to another easy victory, this time 12-0.

It took Canada a little less than five minutes to strike first, Vicky Sunohara driving to the net and knocking home a great pass from the corner by Caroline Ouellette, and two minutes later a similar goal was pushed home by Meghan Agosta from a pass by Gina Kingsbury. Cherie Piper scored short-handed a few minutes later, her first of the Olympics to go with her six assists from last night's 16-0 thrashing of Italy.

Cassie Campbell made another great pass on Canada's fourth goal of the period, feeding Danielle Goyette a back-door beauty that the 40-year-old flag-bearer buried with impressive precision. The Russians responded with a nice give-and-go of their own, Ekaterina Pashkevich getting a good shot on Charline Labonte who made a fine pad save in her Olympics debut.

Piper's second of the game off a faceoff won cleanly by Hayley Wickenheiser made it 5-0. That spelled the end of goalie Irina Gashennikova who had played a good game last night against Sweden but gave up five goals on 16 shots this night. A minute later, Wickenheiser scored short-handed with ridiculous ease at 17:48 to make it an even half dozen. Agosta closed out the first period with a goal on a breakaway to make it 7-0 after just 20 minutes of play.

GAME SUMMARY

First Period

1	Canada, Sunohara (*Ouellette, Goyette*)	4:53
2	Canada, Agosta (*Kingsbury*)	6:52
3	Canada, Piper (*Apps*)	10:00
4	Canada, Goyette (*Campbell*)	15:14
5	Canada, Piper (*Wickenheiser*)	16:18
6	Canada, Wickenheiser (*unassisted*)	17:48
7	Canada, Agosta (*Vaillancourt*)	19:20

penalties: Gavrilova (Rus) 1:14, Agosta (Can) 9:40, Barykina (Rus) 12:06, Pashkevich (Rus) & Apps (Can) 16:09, Kingsbury (Can) 16:25

Second Period

8	Canada, Weatherston (*Ouellette, Vaillancourt*)	7:19
9	Canada, Agosta (*unassisted*)	13:27

penalties: Weatherston (Can) 2:10, Smolina (Rus) 5:08, Petrovskaya (Rus) 12:05, MacLeod (Can) 17:41, Gavrilova (Rus) 18:36

Third Period

10	Canada, Piper (*Wickenheiser*)	1:16
11	Canada, Vaillancourt (*Hefford, Botterill*)	7:47
12	Canada, MacLeod (*Wickenheiser*)	12:33

penalties: Burina (Rus—minor, misconduct) & Khomich (Rus) & Apps (Can) 4:14, Smolina (Rus) 14:27, Botterill (Can) 17:10

In Goal

Canada	Labonte
Russia	Gashennikova/Aleksandrova (16:25, 1st)

Shots on Goal

Canada	19	15	9	**43**
Russia	7	6	4	**17**

Referee	Joy Tottman (GBR)
Linesmen	Johanna Suban (FIN)
	Jana Zitkova (CZE)
Attendance	2,414

Canada's Gina Kingsbury fights for position with Ekaterina Pashkevich.

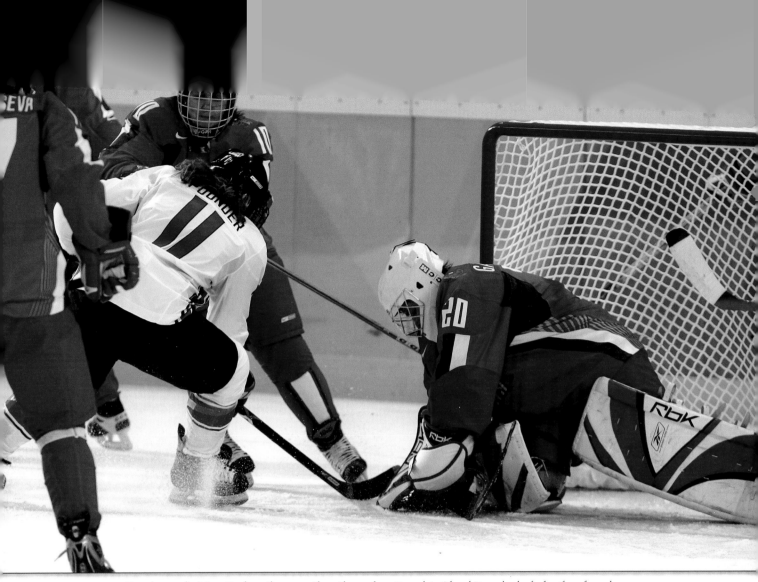

Russian goalie Irina Gashennikova smothers the puck as Canada's Cheryl Pounder looks for the rebound.

It took Canada more than seven minutes in the second to get its eighth goal (Katie Weatherston) and a further six minutes to get number nine, Agosta's third of the game. In between, the Russians had their best performance and had Canada on its heels as the Canadians gave the puck away in their own end and were caught scrambling. Labonte appeared a little rusty in goal, but the team weathered the storm and finished the period strongly.

The third period was anything but lacklustre. Canada scored three more goals, but the Russians became more than a little frustrated by the score and their own play. Tatiana Burina cross-checked Hayley Wickenheiser into the boards from behind and Gillian Apps reciprocated. "Sometimes hits like that are inevitable," Apps rationalized, "but it's natural for someone on our team to stand up, and I was there."

By game's end, the stats rack was full again. Piper and Agosta both had hat tricks, Agosta adding two assists. Wickenheiser had a goal and three assists. ♣

USA 5 / Germany 0

February 12 • Palasport • 7:00 p.m.

The Americans prevailed in their second straight game at the 2006 women's Olympic tournament, but their five-goal margin of victory was hardly convincing.

German netminder Jennifer Harss and her American counterpart Pam Dreyer both got their first starts of the tournament, and Harss was by far the busier of the two as the shots were 60-10 for the Americans.

"I liked the crowd very much," said Harss. "Usually we don't play in front of 8,000 people, so it was a really good atmosphere."

Just 4:33 into the match, Jenny Potter put the Americans up 1-0 on the power play, grabbing a loose puck and flipping a backhander past Harss. With 2:47 left in the first, Katie King tipped home a Julie Chu drive to make it 2-0.

Sarah Parsons got the Americans off to a quick start in the second period, crossing the German blueline on the left side and cutting to the slot to beat Harss with a high wristshot at 1:11.

The Germans rallied with some spirited checking midway through the period, but Parsons killed their momentum when she got loose in the German end and dipsy-doodled her way from the right point to the net. She slid a pass to Natalie Darwitz, who flipped the puck into the open side for a 4-0 lead.

"My thoughts were, I'm going to pass to her no matter what, and the [German] girl sort of overplayed her," said Parsons. "Natalie did a really good job of getting open."

Just past the midway mark of the final period, Parsons put the icing on the cake when she took a short pass from Angela Ruggiero who beat Harss to the glove side.

American forward Kristin King loses the puck to German Denise Soesilo during the second day of games.

Women's Hockey: Players, Coaches, Officials

Canada's Melody Davidson is the only female coach among the eight women's teams in Turin, and all officials are female even though, like players, Europe has a tough time matching talent with the North American officials both in quantity and quality.

The coaching issue is a concern within each federation. The IIHF cannot mandate countries to hire women coaches any more than it can force them to hire specific people for any other position. As with players, the number of people available is the main concern. If Davidson is no longer Canada's coach, Hockey Canada has a deep and rich pool of talent from which to select another woman coach. But even USA Hockey has not had a female head coach since 1995 when Karen Kay led the team. Since then, Ben Smith has been the leader of the American women.

Canada's captain, Cassie Campbell, doesn't see this as an issue within Canada. "We've been lucky because we've had great women coaches over the years, from Mel to Danielle Sauvageau and on down the line. We're really strong in that area."

Dave Fitzpatrick, Sport Director for the IIHF, highlights the coaching dilemma and confirms his governing body can only help from the outside. "We encourage the use of women coaches, but we don't license them and in that case we can't lead by example."

The officials are another story, however. On this point, the IIHF does have complete control, and it does mandate that all officials for women's international hockey are women. Just as the IHF wants to grow the game among players,

Canada's Melody Davidson is the only female coach among the eight women's hockey teams in Turin.

it feels a responsibility to do the same for referees and linesmen.

"Congress made a decision in 1997 that we would use female officials only, and we have encouraged federations to do the same for games within their countries," Fitzpatrick explained. "We have a Development Camp to help with officials, and in this instance we can lead by example. For instance, at the European Women's Champions Cup, we use all female officials."

As a player, Campbell cares only about one thing. "We just want the best person for the job. I don't care if it's male or female. Of course, we want to help develop and grow the game at that level, too, and hopefully we can get some sort of a mentoring program where men can come and work with women to help their development. I think the bottom line is that the game is growing faster than the officials right now."

Sweden 11 / Italy 0

February 13 • Esposizioni • 3:00 p.m.

The 1988 Olympics had Eddie "the Eagle" Edwards, the inept, personable British ski jumper. That same Olympics, in Calgary, also featured the historic bobsled team from Jamaica. Well, 2006 in Turin has its answer to these loveable competitors—the Italian women's hockey team. Led by pint-sized goalie Debora Montanari who, when she was born 25 years ago in Pinerolo, in the foothills of the Italian Alps, could not possibly have guessed she'd be tending the blue ice of a hockey net at the Olympics.

Of course, the Italians got to the five-ringed circus by virtue of their hosting the Olympics, and in their first game they earned the admiration of fans everywhere for showing up and playing 60 minutes as hard as they could. Today's game against the Swedes was an easier test, perhaps, but the outcome—a loss, to be sure—was still to the tune of 11-0. Therese Sjolander led the way with a hat trick.

The Italians got a break when Kim Martin, the sensational Swedish goalie, sat out with a knee injury and the lesser Cecilia Andersson had to play. The goalie matters little, though, when the team mustered fewer shots than the Swedes had goals.

Montanari played a solid game in the first, stopping many shots with good body position, but the first goal by Therese Sjolander was one another goalie might have had.

It was a simple wraparound that went between Montanari's legs, her inexperience in "putting the paddle down," as they say, costing the team one goal. By the end of the first, though, the score was only 3-0, the Swedes hardly playing with the skill or physical tenacity of Canada. Shots were 22-2, which only crystallized the imbalance.

The second period was not as kind to the Italians. They took penalties because of that lack of skill and left Montanari to fend for herself. The result was five more goals to put the score at 8-0.

As with the previous game, coach Markus Sparer inserted backup Luana Frasnelli for the third period, and she acquitted herself much better, allowing just three more goals. But, at the end of the game, the Italian players waved to the crowd in thanks and got a thundering reciprocal ovation.

The chances of the Italians scoring a goal were, well, nil, but their spirit, their very participation, was a celebration of the Olympics in the traditions of Eddie Edwards or that bobsled team from Jamaica. Well worth it.

Italy's Maria Michaela Leitner tries to strip Sweden's Therese Sjolander of the puck. Sjolander had a hat trick in the game.

Finland 4 / Switzerland 0

February 13 • Palasport • 5:30 p.m.

Despite being faster, more skilled, and much better skaters, Finland had its hands full at the Palasport. They defeated the Swiss, as expected, but by a somewhat narrow 4-0 score in the most exciting women's game of the tournament so far. Nonetheless, the Finns have yet to allow a goal so far and the Swiss have yet to score.

The best chance of the early going went to the Finns when Karolina Rantamaki took a long pass up the middle, broke through the defence, and went in alone on goalie Florence Schelling who stood her ground and made a fine save. Stefanie Martie, wearing the unusual number 69 sweater, had a great chance in front of Finnish goalie Noora Ray, but she shot wide and the game remained scoreless.

The lack of skill on the Swiss team showed most frustratingly during a lengthy five-on-three. Despite the two-man advantage, they had trouble even getting into the Finnish end let alone maintaining puck control and generating good scoring chances.

The Finns opened the scoring on their own power play on a beautiful give-and-go between Saara Tuominen and Heidi Pelttari, Pehkonen finishing the sequence off by swiping the puck into the open side of the net.

Switzerland began the second in fine style. The team killed off almost a full two minutes of five-on-three and then had two great scoring chances. On the first, Daniela Diaz went in alone on Raty who made a great glove save on the shot, and on the second, a scramble in front, Silvia Bruggmann couldn't control a loose puck in the crease with Raty down and out.

Indeed, the period belonged to the goalies as this entertaining 20 minutes featured end-to-end rushes, great scoring chances, and a little bit of chippiness for good measure. After 40 minutes, though, it was still a 1-0 game.

Rantamaki, however, displayed her superior skating early in the third when she took a loose puck at centre and simply skated past the Swiss defence. She made a nice move on Schelling to give the Finns a commanding 2-0 lead, and then the floodgates opened. They added two more goals a short time later to put the game out of reach, and at the other end Raty shut the door on the remaining Swiss chances to record the shutout.

Despite the great play of Swiss goalie Florence Schelling, Finland beat Switzerland 4-0 to improve to 2-0-0.

Laura Ruhnke: Switzerland via Toronto

Laura Ruhnke may have been born in Biel, Switzerland, but she speaks with a flawless English accent. "When I speak German, Italian, or French, I have an accent," she said, laughing at the incongruity. As always, however, there's a story that goes with it.

Kent Ruhnke was born in Toronto and grew up playing hockey. As a kid he played for the Ted Reeve Penguins in the MTHL (Metro Toronto Hockey League), and he went on to play at the University of Toronto with the Blues under head coach Tom Watt. Those teams were among the greatest in Canadian university history, and Ruhnke graduated from there to play briefly in the NHL (with Boston) and then two years with the Winnipeg Jets in the WHA.

He ended his career playing in Switzerland and later coaching there (he still does, with Basel). He and his Canadian wife had a child, Laura, in 1983, while they were living in Switzerland. "When I was young, we moved back and forth. We'd spend half the year in Switzerland and the other half in Canada (Toronto)."

Ruhnke took to hockey naturally and developed quickly into a good young player. "When I was in grade nine, I was invited to try out for the B National Team. I played with that team for four years." Her first opportunity to play a game with the Nationals, at age 14 in Japan, was a turning point for her. "I actually decided not to play in that game because that would have made me ineligible for

Laura Ruhnke's father was born in Toronto and played in the NHL, but she made her Olympics debut in 2006 with her adopted homeland of Switzerland.

Canada. But I loved the girls and I felt more Swiss than Canadian, so I played the next year."

Ruhnke went to McGill University in Montreal starting in 2002 to study business, but this year she has been playing for the Lugano Ladies Team, a woman's league which is the top

developmental system in the country. She'll return to McGill in April and then decide whether to finish her degree there or move back to Switzerland. Either way, when she finishes playing she'll settle in her birth country. "My family is in Switzerland, my friends are there. I feel more Swiss."

Canada 8 / Sweden 1

February 14 • Palasport • 3:30 p.m.

Showing superior stick-handling ability and faultless play without the puck, Canada skated to its third straight win in the preliminary round of the women's Olympic tournament by hammering Sweden 8-1 in this loveless Valentine's Day showdown.

That ends the preliminary round for both teams. Canada will now play Finland in one semi-final on February 17 and Sweden faces USA in the other later that day. The winners of those games play for gold.

"We have to be ready for that game," Cheryl Pounder said. "We can't be worried about the score or who we're playing. We just try to take care of business and think of ourselves."

It took Canada a little longer to get going today against an opponent it respected more, but after an early missed chance on the power play, the Canadians pushed an ugly goal past starting goalie Cecilia Andersson who was filling in for the second straight game for Kim Martin. Andersson should have smothered the puck on two or three occasions, but it lay in the crease and Apps got to it first for the early 1-0 lead.

They got their second goal with Bobby Hull-like ferocity. Hayley Wickenheiser skated in over the Swedes' blueline, and with two defencemen to beat she forsook the dipsy-doodle niceties of the deke in favour of the good old fashioned slapshot. She drilled as hard a shot as you'll see in women's hockey past Andersson. The goalie barely moved.

Swedish goalie Cecilia Andersson faced 47 shots and allowed eight goals, but her team only mustered only eight shots all game.

Sweden had two great chances to score one of their own before the end of the period. On one, a sloppy giveaway resulted in Pemilla Winberg at the side of the net, Kim St. Pierre down and out, and the net wide open, but the Swedish forward hit the post and Canada recovered. On the other, a clean faceoff win gave Maria Rooth a direct shot, but she also hit the post.

GAME SUMMARY

First Period

1	Canada, Apps (*unassisted*)	4:36
2	Canada, Wickenheiser (*Pounder*)	12:28

penalties: Lindberg (Swe) 1:29, Apps (Can) 13:24, Sostorics (Can) 14:03, Rundqvist (Swe) 14:55, Wickenheiser (Can) 19:16

Second Period

3	Canada, Apps (*unassistsed*)	3:53
4	Canada, Apps (*Wickenheiser, Piper*)	10:58
5	Canada, Goyette (*Piper, Campbell*)	14:02
6.	Sweden, Lindberg (*Jansson, Winberg*)	16:12
7.	Canada, Weatherston (*Kingsbury*)	17:25
8.	Canada, Botterill (*unassisted*)	18:53

penalties: Lundberg (Swe) 2:21, Apps (Can) 4:57, Pounder (Can) 7:13, Eliasson (Swe) 13:08, Vaillancourt (Can) 14:24, Asserholt (Swe) 17:54, Sunohara (Can) 19:55

Third Period

9	Canada, Goyette (*Piper, Wickenheiser*)	6:02

penalties: Asserholt Swe) 4:20, Andresson (Swe) 17:47

In Goal

Canada	Kim St. Pierre
Sweden	Cecilia Andersson

Shots on Goal

Canada	21	15	11	**47**
Sweden	4	3	1	**8**

Referee	Anu Hirvonen (FIN)
Linesmen	Sanna Mattila (FIN)
	Julie Piacentini (USA)
Attendance	6,850

Gillian Apps scores one of her three goals in an 8-1 rout of Sweden.

Canada made the Swedes pay for their lack of finish by opening a three-goal lead early in the second when Apps swatted in another loose puck in Andersson's crease during a Canadian power play. Wickenheiser set up the fourth goal, Apps's third of the game, with a beautiful pass from behind the net which Apps banged home just past the midway point of the period.

At that point, the game was ostensibly over and only the score remained to be determined. That score was increased when Danielle Goyette tipped in a Cherie Piper slapshot form the point on another power play.

Said Goyette: "I don't think Sweden played their best today. They weren't as physical as they can be and they weren't skating the way we know they can."

Sweden finally got to Canada on a power play of its own at 16:12 when Nanna Jansson's shot was deflected in front by Ylva Lindberg, thus ending Canada's shutout streak that goes back to the 2004 World Championship (Canada lost gold in 2005 in a shootout after not allowing a goal the whole tournament).

Clearly angered, the Canadians responded with a goal of their own less than a minute later as Katie Weatherston scooped in a loose puck to Andersson's back door side. If that weren't enough, Jennifer Botterill tapped in another shot that Andersson fluffed to make it 7-1.

Canada continued unabated in the third period, ignoring USA's Angela Ruggiero's criticisms about running up the score, and added another goal before the final horn.

Referee Anu Hirvonen of Finland called 14 minor penalties in the continuing crackdown on obstruction, but Goyette didn't see that as a worry moving forward. "I think it will be different if we play the U.S. in the finals because the ref knows we're two skilled teams and strong skaters. We're not going to fall down the way players who aren't as strong do."

Wickenheiser was the best player on the ice bar none. Her physical strength, her confidence with the puck, her playmaking, and, of course, that shot, combined to make a marvelous exhibition of the game. ♣

Russia 5 / Italy 1

February 14 • Esposizioni • 1:00 p.m.

Women's hockey had its finest moment of the tournament at 8:02 of the first period of this game during a five-on-three power play for Italy. Maria Michaela Leitner skated down the right side, her off wing, and passed to Sabina Florian in the slot. Florian's wrist shot beat Russian goalie Irina Gashennikova to the short side, and the fans in the stands and players on the Italian bench erupted simultaneously in wild celebration. It gave the Italians a 1-0 lead, their first goal of the tournament after having allowed 26 goals against. It was also their fourth shot of the period after having just nine shots in the previous 120 minutes of play. No matter that Yulia Gladysheva tied the game a couple of minutes later. The tournament goose-egg by the host nation had been cracked.

In fact, the Leitner-Florian combination was effective all period, creating at least three excellent scoring chances for the Italians. The second period was not as kind to them. Russia scored when Svetlana Trefilova deflected a point shot past goalie Debora Montanari to give them a 2-1 lead, and Florian walked in alone on Gashennikova while Italy was short-handed but the goalie made a fine pad save. It was Florian's fourth shot on goal, the same number the entire team had against Sweden the previous day.

The third saw the Russians pull away, but only after the Italians had a long five-on-three that failed to yield a goal. Russia scored three times in the final period to close out the game. In all, four of their five goals were scored on the power play, but Italy left the ice having scored once in the tournament, and in some ways, that counted as much.

Germany 2 / Switzerland 1

February 14 • Esposizioni • 6:00 p.m.

Germany staved off a stubborn Switzerland in the third period of its last game of the round robin this afternoon to win 2-1, its first victory of these 2006 Olympics.

There was no scoring in the opening 20 minutes at the Torino Esposizioni, despite several power play opportunities for both teams. Early in the second period, however, Michaela Lanzl walked in all alone and whipped a wrist shot high over Swiss goalie Patricia Elsmore-Sautter's glove to give the Germans a 1-0 lead.

La Suisse evened the score a few minutes later on a power play when Julia Marty intercepted a clearing attempt off a faceoff in the German end. Her long shot was tipped in front by Tina Schumacher.

The Italians celebrate their first ever goal in women's Olympic hockey.

Finland built an impressive 3-1 lead before surrendering a goal late in the second to allow USA back into the game.

The Germans regained the lead just 36 seconds later when captain Christina Oswald unleashed a slapshot from the blueline that squeezed through Elsmore-Sautter's pads.

Germany kept the pressure on in the third while the Swiss took untimely penalties to kill what momentum they might have hoped to establish. Coach Rene Kamerer pulled Elsmore-Sautter in the final minute, but to no avail. Germany finished the round robin with a 1-2-0 record while the Swiss were winless (0-3-0).

USA 7 / Finland 3

February 14 • Palasport • 8:30 p.m.

Close but no cigar. The Finns were mouth-wateringly close to scoring the biggest upset in women's hockey history. They led USA 3-1 with less than two minutes to go in the second period, but a late power-play goal by Sarah Parsons at 18:54 gave the Americans life heading into the dressing room for the third period. Katie King tied the game less than two minutes into the third, and the Finns collapsed as the Americans came on strong to score what in the end was an easy 7-3 victory.

Mari Pehkonen gave the Finns cause to believe when she scored just 13 seconds into the game. Although the Americans tied the game eight minutes later when Parsons scored on a power play, the Finns skated with the bigger and more skilled USA team and were themselves rewarded again a short time later. Emma Laaksonen beat American goalie Chanda Gunn with an accurate slapshot, and the Finns played with a confidence no one expected.

They continued to take the play to USA in the second and when they made it 3-1 midway through the period, it was clear they were going to give the Americans a run for their money. Parsons' goal late in the period, though, was the turning point in the game and the U.S. turned on the afterburners to win easily. The Finnish Miracle was not to be, at least not on this day, but the way the game was played surely gave Canada some confidence as their closest rivals looked vulnerable for much of the game.

"It was intense, going into the third period," said Ruggiero. "We could have gone two ways, and we just chose to stay composed and use everyone out there. That composure really helped us. And you know what, in the semi-finals, it's great, because if we're down by two goals, we can say, 'Hey, been there, done that.' We can battle back."

Gretzky and Quinn arrive in Turin

"First and foremost, we're here to play at the Olympic Games and represent our country and win a gold medal," Wayne Gretzky said to begin Canada's involvement in Turin.

The 45-year-old head said this year's team would represent an improvement in certain respects over the 2002 gold medal winner. "One thing we have different from '02 is that we understand some of the unknowns, things that may happen or come about. The coaching staff and I, we all understand each other, and we're all on the same page. A lot of the players have played for this country in the past, and we have a little bit more experience than we did in '02. This is a tough tournament, it's a great tournament, and the best players in the world play in it. We believe we have as good a chance to win a gold medal as anyone."

Gretzky defended the selection of a veteran roster despite the impressive NHL performances of youngsters like Sidney Crosby, Eric Staal, and Jason Spezza, saying that the coaching staff wanted to go with "accomplished winners."

Coach Pat Quinn voiced his support for flying the entire Team Canada over as a group, unlike other Olympic teams: "We got together in the summertime for a short camp, and during that time we discussed a lot of the logistics of bringing the team over here."

He added that Canada wouldn't be content to rely on conventional defense. "We'll play an assertive 1-2-2. We'll send our second guy a lot more quickly in a forecheck situation. In the middle of the ice, it'll often be the same sort of thing. We're trying to use our skating and

Wayne Gretzky (with Pat Quinn behind him) talks about Team Canada's chances in Turin.

speed to better advantage. As far as our possession with the puck, we have a basic outline of options off breakouts and mid-ice plays and attack plays. But we're allowing for some freedom for these talented offensive guys to be creative out there, depending on what defenses we see, and we expect a lot of very passive sort of checking from a lot of the teams."

How much will the loss of Norris Trophy-winning defenseman Scott Niedermayer hurt Canada?

"What we lost was a guy who not only could take the attack out and take the pressure off," said Quinn. "We're going to be facing a lot of teams who play a 1-2-2, and he skates through those. We still have some mobile guys, but not like Niedermayer."

Canada 7 / Italy 2

February 15 • Palasport • 1:00 p.m.

Size, speed, skill. Short shifts, pitbull ferocity, and quick ability to adapt to new teammates. All these factors contributed to Canada's brillaint 7-2 win over Italy to start its defence of its 2002 Olympic gold medal.

GAME SUMMARY

First Period

1 Canada, Iginla (Bertuzzi, Sakic)   5:33

penalties: Parco (Ita) 5:09, Borgatello (Ita) 9:03, Ramoser (Ita) & Smyth (Can) 11:47, Trevisani (Ita) 16:55, Heatley (Can) 19:35

Second Period

2 Italy, Cirone (*Scandella*)   0:43
3 Canada, Heatley (*St. Louis, Lecavalier*) 1:55
4 Canada, Doan (*Pronger, Richards*)   5:38
5 Canada, Iginla (*Sakic*)   6:04
6 Canada, St. Louis (*Heatley, Lecavalier*) 13:53
7 Canada, Richards (*Doan, Bertuzzi*)   14:38
8 Italy, Parco (*Tuzzolino*)   18:08

penalties: Trevisani (Ita) 2:49, Nardella (Ita) 5:49, Gagne (Can) 15:27

Third Period

9 Canada, Thornton (*Gagne*)   3:39

penalties: Chittaroni (Ita) 2:28, Foote (Can) 4:28, Ita (too many men) 4:28, Ita (too many men) 5:20, Richards (Can) 9:43, Busillo (Ita) 17:19, Heatley (Can) 18:42

In Goal

Canada	Brodeur
Italy	Muzzatti

Shots on Goal

Canada	11	28	11	**50**
Italy	8	6	6	**20**

Referee	Thomas Andersson (SWE)
Linesmen	Miroslav Halecky (SVK)
	Sergei Shelyanin (RUS)
Attendance	8,575

"We knew they were a quick team and they'd be fired up by their fans," Jarome Iginla said, "so it wasn't an easy game for us at all."

It may have taken the Canadians a few minutes to get their legs, but in the space of about two seconds it was clear things were going to be okay. On an early power play, captain Joe Sakic took the puck down the right side, stopped and passed to Todd Bertuzzi in the corner. He one-timed a pass to Jarome Iginla, and the puck was in and out of the net before the goal light went on. It was a brilliant display of passing and executing, and it gave Canada a 1-0 lead.

Although the first ended with that slim lead, Canada was by far the dominant team. It created the first three power plays of the game, all the result of infractions in the defensive end as the Italians tried to cope with Canada's speed and strength. If Canada was guilty of anything in the period, it was in being too cute in close to goalie Jason Muzzatti, trying to make the perfect pass instead of shooting.

The mostly pro-Italian crowd had something to cheer for early in the second on a power play that carried over from the end of the first. Scandella took a bad-angle shot that was screened in front by Jason Cirone. The puck squirted through Brodeur's pads and the partisan crowd went wild.

Martin St. Louis finishes a beautiful play started by Dany Heatley to give Canada a 5-1 lead in the second period.

The celebrations were short-lived, however, as Canada again scored on a lovely tic-tac-toe play, Dany Heatley finishing off a beautiful pass from Vincent Lecavalier that started with a rush from linemate Martin St. Louis.

They increased their lead to 3-1 thanks to a Shane Doan backhand off a scramble in front of Muzzatti, the puck going in off a defenceman's leg. Iginla made it 4-1 with a great wrist shot after taking another great pass from Sakic, this of the cross-ice variety on a power play. Iginla took the pass, cradled it on his stick like he was shooting targets at the skills event at an All-Star Game, and fired top corner, short side. Bingo.

The pretty plays continued later in the period when Heatley skated over the blueline down the left wing and waited for St. Louis to get to the net before laying a hard, perfect pass across the slot that St. Louis took, held, and flipped into the empty net as Muzzatti played the puck too soon. Another nifty pass less than a minute later, Bertuzzi to Richards, made it 6-1 and more or less salted the win.

The Italians got one back toward the end of the period when defenceman Bryan McCabe lazily swatted the puck with a high stick and left it there for Italian forward Tony Tuzzolino to pick up and drop for John Parco. He made no mistake with a low shot to the far side.

Unlike the Canadian women, the men didn't run up the score in the third. Joe Thornton added a power-play goal, the third of the day on six chances, and Canada coasted the rest of the way to an easy victory.

"Penalties hurt us tonight, for sure," admitted Italian forward Tony Iob. "We played really well in the first, but then we took too many penalties and you can't do that against such a good team."

Iginla praised Hockey Canada for making the transition from NHL to Olympics as smooth as possible. "It's such a quick turnaround, for sure, but we practised together in Toronto and flew here as a team with our families, so we had no worries to distract us. That was really important to us."

"It was good to get off to quick start," Todd Bertuzzi said. Canada next faces Germany tomorrow while the Italians take on Finland earlier in the day. ♣

Captain Joe Sakic bounces off a check and gets back into the play.

Sweden 7 / Kazakhstan 2

February 15 • Esposizioni • 11:30 p.m.

In the opener of the 2006 Olympic men's hockey tournament at the Torino Esposizioni, the Swedes scored three goals on their first nine shots and cruised to a 7-2 win over a lesser team from Kazakhstan.

Keeping roster spots open, Tre Kronor used 18 skaters to Kazakhstan's 20 in the first-ever Olympic meeting between the two countries. Daniel and Henrik Sedin each had a goal and an assist. Daniel Tjarnqvist scored twice, and Daniel Alfredsson, P-J Axelsson,

and captain Mats Sundin also added goals. Yevgeniy Koreshkov and Vladimir Antipin replied for Kazakhstan.

"I thought we played a pretty decent game," said Mattias Ohlund. "It's always tough the first game on the big ice surface. You have to be patient. The Sedins played extremely well, as they have the whole year for us back in Vancouver with the Canucks."

The game featured nice flow in the early going, with very few stoppages in play. The Kazakhs kept the Swedes at bay until 7:45 when Daniel Tjarnqvist backhanded home a rebound from a scrum in front of Yeremeyev's crease for a 1-0 lead.

Daniel Alfredsson scored a great goal a short time later when he knocked defenseman Vladimir Antipin off the puck inside the blueline and fired a wrist shot past Yeremeyev to make it 2-0.

Henrik Sedin was superbly opportunistic on Sweden's 3-0 goal at 16:06, picking up the rebound from a Mikael Samuelsson slapshot before Yeremeyev saw where the puck had dropped.

Just 17 seconds into the second period, Yevgeniy Koreshkov waltzed in alone on Liv and deposited a backhand between the goalie's legs to cut the deficit to 3-1.

Sweden put seven pucks past Kazakh goalie Vitaliy Yeremeyev in the opening game of the men's tournament during an easy 7-2 victory.

Finland's captain Saku Koivu jumps out of the way as a Swiss point shot is on its way to the net.

Finland 5 / Switzerland 0

February 15 • Esposizioni • 3:30 p.m.

Finland played an impressive and poised game in beating Switzerland 5-0 at the Esposizioni tonight. "The most important thing is that our players are ready to play mentally and physically," said Finnish coach Erkka Westerlund.

The Finns not only outplayed the Swiss, they chased starting goalie Martin Gerber from the net and forced coach Ralph Krueger to put David Aebischer in goal for the third period.

"Gerber did not come out because of the score," Krueger offered. "We

just wanted to bring both goalies into the tournament."

Olli Jokinen and Teemu Selanne led the Finns. Each recorded two goals and an assist, and Teppo Numminen had the fifth goal. Three of those goals came with the man advantage.

"They're a great team," said Swiss forward Paul DiPietro. "They've got 17 NHL players on that team. We could do better. We're just going to try to build off our last period, where we improved."

The Finns drew first blood midway through the first with Swiss forward Patrick Fischer in the penalty box. Jokinen's shot from the top of the circle caromed off Swiss defenceman Goran Bezina and eluded Gerber.

The Finns went up 2-0 at 3:35 of the second thanks to some great passing on the power play. Lehtinen spotted Teppo Numminen trailing the play into the Swiss end, and the defenceman snapped a hard wrist shot over Gerber's glove and into the net.

The Finnish power play connected again at 8:04 when Peltonen made a great pass from behind the goal to Jokinen in front, and he quickly redirected it past Gerber.

The brilliant combination of Saku Koivu and Teemu Selanne accounted for the fourth goal, and Selanne picked up a rebound to beat a fallen Gerber for the final score. "We've played together a few times before, so finding that chemistry shouldn't be too tough," said Koivu.

Czech Republic 4 / Germany 1

February 15 • Palasport • 5:00 p.m.

The Germans entered this game against the Czechs, one of the gold-medal contenders, as decided underdogs, and although they succumbed 4-1, they put up a fight few thought they could provide.

The German cause was abetted at 9:25 of the first when Dominik Hasek pulled himself from the net at the whistle. During the previous play, he made what looked like a routine leg save, but he stayed down for a moment as play went out of his end. At the first whistle, he skated to the bench shaking his head, and he was replaced by Tomas Vokoun.

The Germans got the opening goal on a power play They won a faceoff in the Czech end, and the point shot by Alexander Sulzer was brilliantly deflected by Tino Boos in front past a helpless Vokoun.

"They played really well in the first period," Jagr agreed. "But it was difficult for us. We haven't even had one practise together, and it takes time. We were tired. It's not as easy as you think. We play 60 games in one style and ice size and then we come here and have to change so much."

Just 1:02 after the faceoff to start the second, defenceman Tomas Kaberle blew into the German zone down the right side and scored on Kolzig through his legs to tie the game. They went ahead for good at 3:38 on a brilliant pass from the corner by Martin Straka to Kaberle again who was pinching in from the point on a Czech power play. He beat Kolzig through the five-hole again to make it 2-1.

Midway through the third, Milan Hejduk was hooked after taking a breakaway pass. Referee Marouelli immediately pointed to centre ice—a penalty shot—and on the attempt Kolzig outwaited Hejduk and forced him to shoot high. The save kept the Germans just one shot away from a tie.

Alas, that shot never came and the miracle had to wait. With three minutes to go, Jagr took a harmless shot that Kolzig blocked, but the puck bounced off a defender and into the net for the all-important insurance goal. David Vyborny added the final goal into the empty net.

Despite his third-period goal, Jaromir Jagr had a quiet game in his team's 4-1 win over Germany.

Slovakia 5 / Russia 3

February 15 • Esposizioni • 8:00 p.m.

Marian Gaborik broke a 3-3 third period tie with two dazzling goals to give Slovakia a surprise 5-3 victory over Russia.

With 3:28 remaining, the Minnesota Wild speedster grabbed a loose puck at centre ice, roared down the right side and beat goalie Ilya Bryzgalov with a snap shot that gave the Slovaks a 4-3 lead. Then, in the final minute of play, he outraced the Russian defencemen down the left side and drilled a sensational wrist shot high over the goalie to make the win more emphatic.

"I try to go out there and skate," said Gaborik. "That's my big thing. I try to create chances for myself and my teammates."

From the opening faceoff to the final horn, the pace was breakneck and the scoring chances many in what was a showcase of speed and skill. The Slovaks opened the scoring at 9:07 when Marian Hossa tore down the right side and fed a saucer pass to Pavol Demitra. He wasted no time in snapping a shot top shelf to the far side.

The Russians tied the game less than a minute later when Pavel Datsyuk took a lovely pass from Danny Markov and made a great deke in tight on goalie Peter Budaj.

The top Russian threesome of Datsyuk-Ilya Kovalchuk-Alexei Kovalev put their team in front at 12:38 of the first, Kovalev finishing the rush with a great one timer in the slot that Budaj didn't have a chance on.

A Darius Kasparaitis penalty early in the second gave the Slovaks their chance to get back into the game. Lubomir Visnovsky drilled a shot under the crossbar off a faceoff win at 5:51 and the Slovak contingent in the crowd went wild.

Russia took a 3-2 lead a short time later on its own power play when Alexander Ovechkin tipped a Sergei Gonchar point shot through Budaj's legs.

The third power-play goal of the period tied the game for the Slovaks again. Andrei Meszaros's point shot dribbled through Bryzgalov's pads, and Peter Bondra pushed it the final few inches over the goal line before the goalie could cover up.

The third period was chock full of end-to-end rushes, long periods without whistles, and great goaltending. Gaborik's heroics were fitting end to a game either team might have won. In the end, his brilliant play in the clutch proved the difference.

"It was a very high-speed game, with lots of good scoring chances on both sides, and a physical game as well," said Slovak defenceman Zdeno Chara.

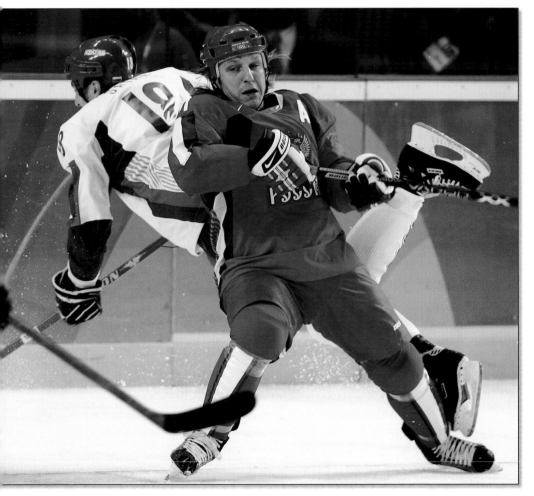

Darius Kasparaitis does what he does best—takes his man (Miroslav Satan) out of the play.

Latvia 3 / USA 3

February 15 • Palasport • 9:00 p.m.

The Latvians and Americans began their Olympics by playing to a fun and entertaining 3-3 tie.

"It's definitely a rude awakening," Bill Guerin said after coming off the ice, disappointed. "We're going to have to get a lot better. But at the same time, they're a good team and they worked hard."

USA got on the board first on the power play when John-Michael Liles made a perfect pass to Brian Gionta streaking through the high slot. His pinpoint wrist shot beat Arturs Irbe high over the blocker side. A minute later, the Americans struck again when a routine shot by Craig Conroy slipped under the arm of the diminutive Latvian goaler to give USA an early and impressive 2-0 lead.

The Latvians struck back as they converted a three-on-two when Aleksandrs Semjenovs dropped the puck to Sandis Ozolins. His shot was stopped by John Grahame, but the rebound came right to Aleksandrs Nizivijs who had the open net. That was all the scoring in what was an entertaining, fast period in which the Latvians had the edge in play.

Midway through the second, the Latvians started to be more assertive on the rush. Latvia tied the game on a power play at 15:04 when a quick shot by Atvars Tribuncovs made its way through about half a dozen bodies in front of Grahame and past the screened goalie. Less than a minute later, Herberts Vasiljevs burst down the left side and the right-handed shot ripped a great blast to the far side over the glove of Grahame. The stunned Latvian crowd exploded with joy, and the once confident Americans were clearly on their heels.

Early in the third, the tide turned again. Irbe surrendered another weak goal when he flubbed a long point shot from Jordan Leopold that wasn't screened. The goal produced a more cautious approach to the rest of the period as neither team wanted to make the mistake that cost the team two points in the standings.

Mike Knuble suggested it might have been a good thing to gain a point and lose one at the same time. "It sure changes the dynamics of how we approach the rest of the tournament. It turns the screw a bit, but maybe that's a good thing. Maybe we'll play better if we're forced to."

Diminutive Latvian goaltender, veteran Arturs Irbe, makes a melodramatic save during the first period of his team's 3-3 tie with USA.

The Men Arrive — Some Remain Home

As the men prepared for a full slate of games, virtually all of the top teams in Torino suffered roster troubles because of injuries and withdrawals from competition.

Canada was hard hit in losing defencemen Ed Jovanovski and Scott Niedermayer to injury. They were replaced by Bryan McCabe and Jay Bouwmeester. Jovanovski recently underwent abdominal surgery and Niedermayer opted for surgery rather than risk further damage to his sore knee. McCabe, meanwhile, was himself just getting back to action after missing nearly a month with a slight groin tear . He was called in to replace Jovanovski.

Finland, meanwhile, was decimated. It lost seven players named to the team just before Christmas, starting with its top two goalies, Miikka Kiprusoff of Calgary and Atlanta's Kari Lehtonen. The pair of padded puckstoppers earned the wrath of their homeland fans for withdrawing in order to rest up for the drive to the Stanley Cup in NHL play. Although both were nursing injures leading up to Torino, they were also playing regularly for their club teams. Back home, their loyalty and courage were questioned. Additionally, Sami Kapanen, Tuomo Ruutu, and Ossi Vaananen (broken foot) also withdrew. Later, Joni Pitkanen and Antti Miettinen also suffered injuries.

The Swedes suffered a significant blow when star forward Markus Naslund pulled out because of a nagging groin injury. He had been playing nightly for Vancouver but decided to skip the Olympics to rest his body. The

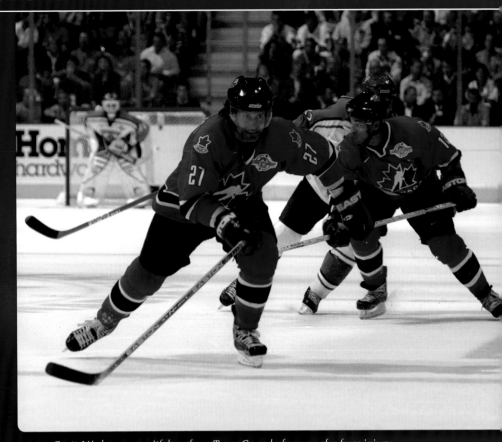

Scott Niedermayer withdrew from Team Canada because of a knee injury.

oft-injured Foppa, Peter Forsberg, went to Turin but missed the first two games to rest his weary bones. Kim Johnsson and Nicklas Kronwall also had to pull out. Kronwall later played for Sweden.

Slovakia's Ladislav Nagy was out for the year with a legitimate and serious knee injury suffered while playing for the Phoenix Coyotes, and the small hockey power also had to contend with the surprise retirement of Ziggy Palffy in mid-January.

The Russians lost several players as well. Goalie Nikolai Khabibulin, who in the past

has refused to participate in international tournaments for Russia, withdrew because of an injured MCI that required weeks of recovery, as did Boston's Alexei Zhamnov. Additionally, they were minus Alexei Zhitnik, Dmitri Bykov, and Denis Kulyash.

The Czechs lost only Petr Prucha and replaced him with Patrik Elias. The Americans, considered underdogs, lost only defenceman Aaron Miller, who was quickly replaced by Bret Hedican.

In all, more than 20 players named to their teams withdrew before the first drop of the puck.

Canada 5 / Germany 1

February 16 • Palasport • 8:00 p.m.

Canada's 5-1 win over Germany was a routine and expected result, unlike at Salt Lake City four years ago when Canada squeaked out a 3-2 win. Roberto Luongo got the start for Canada and faced only a dozen shots, but he was also a little lucky in that the Germans hit the post three times and another shot by Daniel Kreutzer slipped through his pads and just wide of the empty net.

NHL goalie and Canadian-raised Olaf Kolzig was the surprise backup as German coach Uwe Krupp went with Thomas Greiss, who represents the country's future in the crease.

"He has dreams about playing in the NHL, and the Olympic Games are a lot about dreams," said Krupp. "This young goaltender has played terrific and elevated his game. I think he deserved this start with the spotlight on him."

"He played well," said Chris Pronger of Greiss. "We had a five-on-three for about a minute and a half in the second period, and he came up with some huge saves. There was a pass across the crease to Joe [Sakic], and I thought he had an empty net, but the goalie got his pad across."

Ultimately, the Germans just couldn't keep up with Canada, especially as it was playing without injured stars Marco Sturm and Jochen Hecht. They also took nine minor penalties, most the result of

Canada's Martin St. Louis watches action from the bench.

superior Canadian speed and skill.

"Playing without Marco Sturm and Jochen Hecht is comparable, for us, to Canada playing without Mario and Wayne," Krupp admitted.

Canada opened the scoring at 4:52 after almost surrendering the

GAME SUMMARY

First Period

1	Canada, Redden (*Gagne, Thornton*)	4:52
2	Canada, Sakic (*Bertuzzi, Nash*)	7:29
3	Canada, Gagne (*Regehr, Richards*)	10:49

penalties: Pronger (Can) 1:00, Felski (Ger) 6:24, Heatley (Can) 9:43, Kreutzer (Ger) 10:14, Sulzer (Ger) 12:08, Martinec (Ger) 15:16, Lecavalier (Can) 19:42

Second Period

4	Germany, Ehrhoff (*Schubert, Ustorf*)	9:13
5	Canada, Heatley (*Foote*)	5:37

penalties: Ehrhoff (Ger) 3:49, McCabe (Can) 6:59, Pronger (Can) 7:15, Busch (Ger) 7:43, Busch (Ger) 13:08, Ehrhoff (Ger) 13:26

Third Period

6	Canada, Doan (*Smyth*)	19:26

penalties: McCabe (Can--minor, misconduct) 2:23, Nash (Can) 7:01, Seidenberg (Ger) 14:31

In Goal

Canada	Luongo
Germany	Greiss

Shots on Goal

Canada	9	18	13	**40**
Germany	2	6	4	**12**

Referee	Christer Larking (SWE)
Linesmen	Miroslav Halecky (SVK)
	Thor Eric Nelson (USA)
Attendance	8,554

Joe Sakic knocks in the rebound off a Rick Nash shot to give Canada a 2-0 lead early in the game.

first goal just seconds earlier. Germany's Eduard Lewandowski chased down a loose puck as it headed toward Luongo, but the goalie came well out of his net to try to get there first. In the end, it was Lasse Kopitz who got there first, but as he

shot into the empty net, Canadian defenceman Adam Foote slid across the crease and made a great save in Luongo's absence. The Canadians turned the puck up ice, and Simon Gagne made a fine pass to Wade Redden who counted the first goal.

Canada went up 2-0 on the power play. Todd Bertuzzi barrelled down the right side into the German zone and made a drop pass to Rick Nash. Greiss blocked the shot, but Joe Sakic picked up the rebound and shoved it in.

At 10:49, Gagne made it 3-0 with a determined charge to the net, getting his stick on a Brad Richards rebound even as defender Rob Leask checked him to the ice.

The Germans hit the post for the first time when Marcel Goc deflected a Dennis Seidenberg shot

past Luongo. The Germans got on the board at 9:13 of the second when Christoph Schubert slid a beautiful pass from behind the net to Christian Ehrhoff in the slot. Ehrhoff drilled a great shot over Luongo's glove, and the power-play goal made it 3-1.

The Canadians restored their three-goal lead a few minutes later when Dany Heatley batted in a rebound off the end boards while fending off a check. Video replay confirmed it was not swatted with a high stick. Shane Doan finished the scoring in the last minute of the game after Canada coasted through the third.

German fans are among Europe's most vocal, but they were outnumbered by the sea of red-garbed Canadians at the Palasport Olympico among the crowd of 8,554. ♣

Simon Gagne falls after scoring Canada's third goal of the first to give the team a commanding lead.

Finland 6 / Italy 0

February 11 • Palasport • 12:00 p.m.

A day after hammering Switzerland, the Finns scored another shutout win, this a 6-0 whitewash of Italy. Five of those goals came from the power play.

The hometown crowd roared every time the Italians managed to carry the puck into the neutral zone, but Giorgio de Bettin had Italy's only good scoring chances of the first period.

The Finns broke the scoreless tie 1:49 into the second with the man advantage when Jere Lehtinen pushed in a Teppo Numminen shot that rolled along the goal line. Two minutes later, Saku Koivu scored a lucky goal when an intended pass bounced off an Italian defenceman and into the net.

"We knew we were going to find a way to score," Teemu Selanne said. "We just had to keep our legs moving and get some more power plays. When you get one or two, it opens up and the goals come a little easier."

Midway through the game, the Italians lost their composure and took a series of needless penalties. Mario Chitarroni's double minor for elbowing and boarding at 7:14 was a notable example. A this point, coach Michel (Mickey) Goulet called a timeout to try to gather his troops. Goalie Gunther Hell made a fine glove save on a point shot from Aki Berg, but he couldn't stop Jussi Jokinen's deflection of a Petteri Nummelin shot at 10:11 that made it 3-0 Finland.

Kimmo Timonen drove a shot off Hell's left post, but before the period ended the Finns converted again. Ville Peltonen made it 4-0 with a high blast stick side at 18:25. All four goals were scored with the man advantage.

The Finns outscored their first two opponents by a combined 11-0.

On a third-period five-on-three for Finland, Selanne converted a Koivu pass at the side of the net at 12:07. He then added his second of the game with a one-timer on a give-and-go with Jere Lehtinen at 15:10. The latter was Finland's only even-strength goal.

"We just have to put the first two games aside," said Selanne. "We know we have to play better as a team as the tournament goes on. We know the Czechs very well, too, so I think it's going to be a good match."

"The five power play goals killed us," Italian forward Tony Iob said. "We hung in there in the first period, and then, like the first game, it came down to penalties. If we don't get called on too many penalties, it prolongs our chances.

Switzerland 3 / Czech Republic 2

February 16 • Esposizioni • 1:00 p.m.

David Aebischer's goaltending, the Swiss penalty killing, and a third-period power-play goal from Mark Streit to break a 2-2 tie proved the difference as the Swiss stunned the Czechs 3-2.

The Swiss scored the game's first goal after Jaroslav Spacek was stripped of the puck in front of his goalie Tomas Vokoun. Ivo Ruthemann took a hard slapshot that trickled through Vokoun's pads and rolled in the crease, and Ruthemann swiped the loose puck into the open net to give the Swiss a stunning 1-0 lead to the delight of their fans.

The Swiss confidence took a major hit at 2:55 of the second when they turned the puck over inside their line. Martin Straka made a great saucer pass about two feet off the ice that landed softly on Jaromir Jagr's stick in the slot, and he roofed a high shot over Aebischer's blocker to tie the game 1-1.

At 9:44, Thierry Paterlini scored the best goal of the tournament to date. Short-handed, he simply skated slowly into the Czech end with the puck trying to kill time. Surrounded by four Czechs, he was almost stationary when Spacek checked him off the puck and knocked him down. But no Czech bothered to claim the puck or watch the fallen Swiss forward, and Paterlini got up, collected the disc, and went in alone on a stunned Vokoun who was fooled by Paterlini's weak backhand. The defensive lapse, the error again by Spacek, the poor goaltending, the short-handed effort, all made for a perfect goal.

"I was a little surprised the puck was still available," Paterlini said after. "But I just got up and tried to take as hard a shot as I could. Lucky for me, it went in."

The Swiss then ran into serious penalty trouble as NHL referee Dennis LaRue had the Czechs on a five-on-three for more than a minute, and while that was in progress he called another minor on the Swiss. That's when goalie Aebischer battened the hatches of his cord cage and made a series of highlight-reel saves.

The magic appeared to come to an end early in the third when Rastislav Olesz one-timed a shot to Aebischer's stick side to tie the game once again.

The Swiss then did what the Czechs had failed to do—score with the man advantage. Mark Streit simply took a pass at the point and blasted a hard shot over the glove of Vokoun. That shot won the game.

Mark Streit blasts the game-winning goal past Tomas Vokoun in the third period.

Russia 5 / Sweden 0

February 16 • Palasport • 4:00 p.m.

Russia scored three goals in the second period en route to a convincing 5-0 win over Sweden.

"Up until their second goal, I think we were doing okay," said Swedish captain Mats Sundin. "When you turn the puck over in the neutral zone like we did against these kinds of forwards, you're shooting yourself in the foot."

Alexei Kovalev, Alexander Ovechkin, Maxim Sushinsky, Viktor Kozlov, and Maxim Afinogenov scored for Russia, with every line contributing. It was Russia's first-ever shutout against Sweden at the Olympics.

"It was the wrong team to have a bad day against," said goalie Henrik Lundqvist.

A rift apparently developed between Ilya Bryzgalov, who played goal in Russia's opening 5-3 loss to Slovakia, and Russian head coach Vladimir Krikunov, who said in praise of Nabokov after this game: "The most important thing is that we changed the goaltender. Yesterday, I can say it was my mistake that Bryzgalov was the main goaltender." Krikunov added that Maxim Sokolov would serve as Nabokov's backup, since Bryzgalov did not "understand" his coach.

After a scoreless first period, Alexei Kovalev opened the scoring for Russia at 7:13 with a tremendous slapshot from the faceoff circle to Lundqvist's right that beat the goalie glove side.

At 8:05, the Russians jumped into a 2-0 lead when Alexander Ovechkin grabbed the rebound from an Alexei Yashin slot drive and deposited it past a prone Lundqvist.

With 1:02 left in the second period, the Russians went up 3-0 on a super passing play off the rush, and it was the Super Leaguers coming through, as Sergei Zhukov dropped the puck to Malkin, who fed Sushinsky to Lundqvist's right for a tap-in.

Early in the third period, the Swedes thought they'd broken Nabokov's goose egg. Mats Sundin went hard to the net and knocked over the goalie as Nicklas Lidstrom backhanded the puck into the empty net. But the Tre Kronor captain was penalized for interference, and the goal was disallowed.

At 10:31, Viktor Kozlov one-timed an Alexander Frolov feed under the crossbar to make it 4-0, killing off any Swedish hopes of a comeback.

Maxim Afinogenov rounded out the scoring with his best Pavel Bure imitation with 5:06 remaining, coming out of the penalty box, taking a long feed from Pavel Datsyuk, and sprinting in to slide a backhand between Lundqvist's legs.

Russia's Maxim Afinogenov and Sweden's P-J Axelsson collide as Alexei Yashin skates by.

Slovakian captain Pavol Demitra celebrates with Andrej Meszaros and Marian Hossa.

Slovakia 6 / Latvia 3

February 16 • Esposizioni • 5:00 p.m.

The dazzling display of breathtaking speed and high-octane skill of the Slovaks proved no match for the Latvians. The 6-3 final score reflected well the superiority in skill of the winning side.

"We didn't play a good 60 minutes the way we did yesterday against Russia, but we still are pleased with the result," captain Pavol Demitra said. "We opened up too much and played their game, which we didn't want to do."

At 5:23, Richard Zednik stepped in over the blueline and, using Rodrigo Lavins as a screen, ripped a shot high over Irbe's glove, sending the Slovak fans into a frenzy. Just 20 seconds later they made it 2-0 when Ronald Petrovicky was sent in all alone down the wing and with the puck rolling he beat Irbe through the five-hole.

Not to be outdone, Sandis Ozolins took a pass to the point on the next shift, moved in two strides to the top of the faceoff circle, and drilled the puck under the blocker arm of Jan Lasak at 6:27 to cut the lead in half.

Playing like goals were a dime a dozen, the Slovaks went up by two again while playing short-handed. Marian Hossa burst down the right wing with a blaze of speed on a two-on-one. He waited for the streaking Pavol Demitra to reach the net, flipped the puck in front, and watched as his teammate deflected it into the open side of the goal.

Hossa scored again on another lightning rush. While he bolted down the right side again, everyone was watching Marian Gaborik tear through the middle. Hossa simply held on to the puck and beat Irbe cleanly.

"You see guys like Gaborik and Hossa skate, and they're the fastest players in the NHL. That's the kind of game they play," Demitra added.

"That's our game, for sure," Lubos Bartecko agreed. "We like to get turnovers and then attack their goal with our speed."

The Latvians connected on a power play early in the second when Aigars Cipruss made a fine pass from behind the net to Martins Cipulis who snapped the one-timer past Lasak's glove.

Soon after, Karlis Skrastins made the luckiest pass you'll ever see as it bounced and hopped over two Slovak sticks right onto Skrastins's stick. He broke in alone on Lasak and roofed a backhand on the deke to make it a 4-3 game.

Zdeno Chara and Hossa finished the scoring for the Slovaks.

USA 4 / Kazakhstan 1

February 16 • Esposizioni • 9:00 p.m.

It may have gotten the job done, but this pedestrian 4-1 win by USA over Kazkahstan was hardly a work of art. Nonetheless, it gave the Americans their first win of the Olympics and put them on firmer footing for advancing to the quarter-finals next week.

"We're supposed to beat these teams," Brian Rolston said, "but we played with confidence tonight and we have another day under our belt."

The Kazakhs' hopes of replicating the 4-3 upset by the Swiss of the Czechs earlier in the day at Esposizioni were dashed just 94 seconds after the opening faceoff when Chris Drury passed to Bill Guerin at the top of the faceoff circle and number 13 rifled a pinpoint shot over the shoulder of Vitaliy Kolesnik to give the Americans an early lead.

USA made it 2-0 just nine seconds after the start of a power play when Brian Rolston teed up a pass from Doug Weight and drilled a low shot past Yeremeyev at 8:31.

The Americans continued to pound away the rest of the period, using their superior size and skills to advantage while goalie Rick DiPietro stood mostly idle 200 feet away. They were rewarded a third time, again with the extra skater, when Brian Gionta tipped in a point shot by John-Michael Liles while Keith Tkachuk caused havoc in front of the Kazakh goalie.

Target practice continued in the second as shift after American shift came in on Yeremeyev, creating good scoring chances or drawing obstruction penalties. Indeed, the Kazakhs' best scoring chance came when a loose puck rolled out to centre just as Artyom Argokov came out of the penalty box, but he shot well wide on the partial breakaway.

Not that this was going to start a comeback by any stretch, but the Kazakhs showed some pluck in the third and the Americans grew more and more frustrated by their inability to score, even on the power play (2-9). Midway through, Yevgeniy Koreshkov redirected a point shot with Keith Tkachuk in the penalty box to make it 3-1, but then, as if awakened, Mike Modano came right back on a give-and-go to make it 4-1 USA.

"We spent too much time in the penalty box against Latvia and I think we did a much better job of staying out of there tonight," Chelios added.

Kazakhstan's Oleg Kovalenko chases a loose puck in the corner of the Torino Esposizioni arena.

Canada's Other Canadian Players

While the players wearing the red and white of Team Canada started their quest for a gold medal, Canada was represented at the Olympic hockey venues by no fewer than 12 other hockey players in the men's tournament, Canadian-born but playing for other countries. Atop that list was the Italian contingent, of which nine were Canadians. Additionally, there was Laura Ruhnke, daughter of Toronto-born and former NHL player, Kent Ruhnke, who plays for the Swiss national team, and Ralph Krueger, the Swiss men's coach who was born and raised in Winnipeg.

The Italo-Canadians include Joe Busillo of Toronto who played junior with the Oshawa Generals in the late 1980s. He couldn't get a chance in the NHL and moved quickly to Italy, and he has been playing in Europe ever since.

Mario Chittaroni has played in eight World Championships for Italy starting in 1992. A native of tiny Haileybury, Ontario, he is an Italian citizen long removed from his northern Ontario roots.

Toronto native Jason Cirone was drafted by the Winnipeg Jets in 1989, but he played only three games with his Jets, his only NHL time. He played for several years in minor pro in North America after an initial foray to Italy, but since 2001 his has been an exclusively Italian career with Asiago.

Paul Di Pietro is a name more familiar in Canada. He was born in the Soo and had a traditional NHL career, playing junior, then moving to the minors, and finally establishing himself with the Montreal Canadiens in 1991. He later played for Toronto, his only two stops in a 192-game NHL

career, and after several more years in the minors he decided to give Switzerland a chance. Di Pietro has been there ever since, but 2006 marks his Olympic debut with La Suisse.

Tony Iob, originally from Renfrew, Ontario, has also played for Italy for years. He has been playing in Europe since 1993 and has played at three World Championships for Italia—1997, 1998, and 2001.

Mike Knuble of the USA was born in Toronto where his Canadian father and American mother started a family. He went on to play university hockey in Michigan and has represented USA on several occasions, most recently the 2005 World Championship.

Robert Leask is in Turin playing for the Germans, but he was born in Toronto. He played for Germany at the 2004 World Championship.

Goalie Jason Muzzatti of Toronto was drafted by Calgary back in the Olympic year of 1988, and he played parts of six seasons in the NHL before moving to Europe in 1998.

John Parco played parts of three seasons in the minors in North America after being selected a distant 248th overall by Philadelphia in 1991. Other than that, he has played in Europe, mostly Asiago, Italy, and as such he was with the Italians for these Olympics.

Giulio Scandella is just 22 years old, but after a junior career in the

Tony Iob is one of nine Italo-Canadians at the 2006 Olympics.

Quebec league he moved to Asiago in 2003 and has been there since. The Olympics marks his major international debut with the team.

Andre Signoretti has played with Fassa in the Italian league for the last four seasons. Carter Trevisani of Carlisle, Ontario, was drafted by Carolina in 2001 but after two more years with the Ottawa 67's he signed with the Varese hockey club.

So, Canada has its 23-player roster for the men's and women's teams, but it is also represented in Italy, Germany, Switzerland, and USA. Truly, the home of hockey has shared its wealth with the world.

Canada 6 / Finland 0

February 17 • Palasport • 9:00 p.m.

While the Americans were on the ice in the early afternoon losing a shocking shootout to Sweden, Canada's women were in the runways down behind the ice running lightly, stretching, and preparing for their late date with Finland for the other place in the gold-medal game. If looks could kill, those players looked like a team of John Waynes. And, if there were any doubt about Canada

Canada continued to score goals at will, putting six more past Finland to bring their total to 42 in just four games.

taking Finland lightly--despite never having lost to the Finns, despite having the vastly superior team--that early Sweden-USA result drove home in Melody Davidson's dressing room the fact that any thing can happen and sometimes it does.

Tonight, though, it didn't. Canada played a virtually mistake-free game and beat Finland 6-0 before a crowd of 7,306 at Palasport to advance to Monday night's gold-medal game. Finland will now play USA for the bronze medal earlier that day.

"We watched a bit of the game earlier, and then when we got to the arena, we watched the shootout," Jennifer Botterill said. "It was an exciting finish, but we feel for the U.S. because we know a lot of girls on that team."

It was fully half a period before Canada got its legs and started asserting itself. Caroline Ouellette made a nice rush down the right side on a power play, only to be stopped by Maija Hassinen in the Finnish

net, but a Gillian Apps high sticking penalty put a premature end to that man advantage.

As the period wore on, a patient Canada started to gain the upper hand and took the play to Finland. The team was finally rewarded at 17:33 on the power play. Katie Weatherston, who had done a great job killing a penalty a few minutes earlier, took the puck out of the corner, and skated in front unmolested. She drilled a wrist shot under the blocker arm of Hassinen for the first goal to get the team over that psychological hump of a second possible Miracle at Palasport today.

They connected again at 19:15 on another power play, this time Gillian Apps taking a bad-angle shot to Hassinen's left. She made the save but Danielle Goyette was right there to pop in the rebound. The late-period surge put Canada in the driver's seat heading to the dressing room.

Canada's improved play from the end of the first developed in the

GAME SUMMARY

First Period

| 1 | Canada, Weatherston (*Sostorics*) | 17:33 |
| 2 | Canada, Apps (*Kingsbury, Goyette*) | 19:15 |

penalties: Botterill (Can) 3:24, Mertanen (Fin) 10:53, Apps (Can) 12:19, Parvianen (Fin) 15:40, Saarinen (Fin) 19:05, Palvila (Fin) 19:39

Second Period

| 3 | Canada, Wickenheiser (*Apps*) | 4:59 |
| 4 | Canada, Ouellette (*Sunohara*) | 6:26 |

penalties: Wickenheiser (Can) 8:02, Mertanen (Fin) 13:58, Sirvio (Fin) 16:00, Pounder (Can) 18:41

Third Period

| 5 | Canada, Piper (*Wickenheiser, Apps*) | 7:49 |
| 6 | Canada, Piper (*Wickenheiser, Apps*) | 14:47 |

penalties: Pounder (Can) 3:41, Apps (Can) 8:14, Goyette (Can) 9:38, Tuominen (Fin) 10:23, Kovalainen (Fin) 12:57

In Goal

| Canada | | | | Labonte |
| Finland | | | Hassinen/Raty (16:26 2nd) | |

Shots on Goal

| Canada | 12 | 12 | 16 | **40** |
| Finland | 5 | 5 | 7 | **17** |

Referee	Danyel Howard (USA)
Linesmen	Julie Piacentini (USA)
	Klara Quagliato (CZE)

| Attendance | 7,306 |

second into meticulous, methodical hockey. The team's defence was simply impenetrable, and Labonte really did not have to face any tough shots. Canada broke out of its end with effective authority, carried the play to the Finns much of the time, and seemed, unlike USA, in no danger of surrendering or compromising that 2-0 lead.

Canada made it 3-0 almost effortlessly, on a power play, when Hayley Wickenheiser lofted a wrist shot at the goal through a maze of players. It floated past the screened Hassinen without being touched, and Wickenheiser had her 13th point of the tournament, tops among the women.

They added a fourth goal at 16:26 when another point shot, this a true slapshot from Caroline Ouellette which slipped through Hassinen's pads. It was a shot the goalie should have stopped, and the 4-0 advantage signaled the end of any real hopes the Finns might have had of winning. Saintula more or less agreed, for he replaced his starting goalie with backup Noora Raty.

Much of the third passed as uneventfully. Canada moved the puck out quickly, dumped the puck deep in the Finnish end and chased it down, and took short, energetic shifts.

The lead extended to five goals courtesy of a nice pass at the top of the crease by Wickenheiser to Cherie Piper who roofed a shot over Raty's shoulder. A few minutes later, Piper replicated that shot to make it an even half dozen on the night.

"They battled us five-on-five, and special teams definitely played a part in the win," Canadian coach Melody Davidson noted. "Everyone stuck to the game plan."

Canada will be prohibitive favourites to beat Sweden and retain its Olympic crown, having hammered Domkronor 8-1 just a few short days ago. "I think the U.S. has a lot of great players," Saara Tuominen offered, "but Canada is a more complete team." ♣

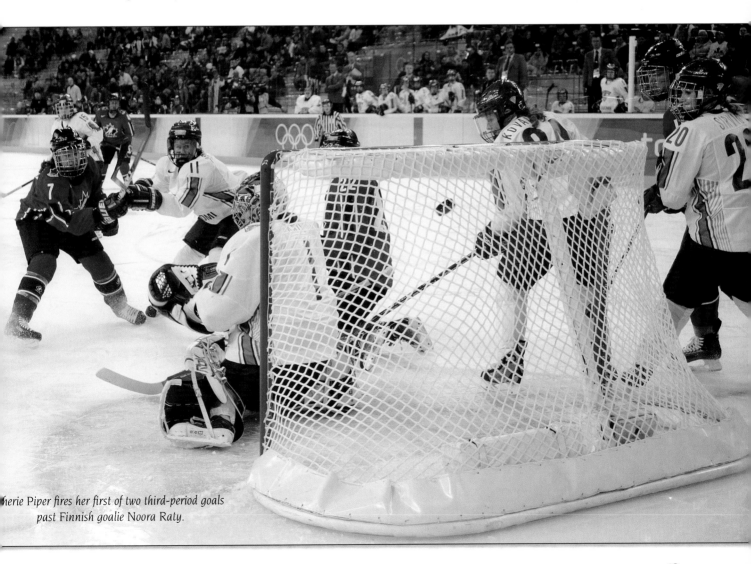

Cherie Piper fires her first of two third-period goals past Finnish goalie Noora Raty.

Sweden 3 / USA 2 (OT/SO)

February 17 • Palasport • 5:00 p.m.

Do you believe in Swedish miracles? Posting the greatest upset in the history of women's hockey, Sweden rallied from a 2-0 deficit to defeat USA in a shootout (2-0) and earn one place in the gold-medal game. This marked the first time a European nation had ever defeated Canada or USA in Olympic or World Championship competition.

The heroes for Sweden were few. At the top of the list was goalie Kim Martin who faced 39 shots in regulation and then blanked the Americans on their four shots in the shootout. Right after her came the incredible Maria Rooth who scored

both goals in the second period to tie the game and added the shootout clincher. She logged more ice time than any player in the game. And then there was 16-year-old Pernilla Winberg who scored the shootout winner when she skated directly in on goalie Chanda Gunn and drilled a low shot stick side with a goalscorer's knack. Next in line were the Swedish penalty killers who killed off eleven penalties in total, including one crucial five-on-three and one penalty in overtime.

"We practiced the shootout lots of times before the Olympics," said the 16-year-old Winberg. "We talked about winning a lot, and we thought that anything could happen, so we went out and tried to win the game."

"I can't believe it," said Martin. "This is awesome. I felt good all game,

not nervous at all. We've watched the movie Miracle many times, and I always imagine that I am Jim Craig."

"Kim Martin saved the game for us with her brilliant saves," said Swedish head coach Peter Elander.

Natalie Darwitz took the USA's first shootout attempt but hit the post. Erika Holst missed for Sweden when she tried to replicate Peter Forsberg's famous winning move at the 1994 Olympics versus Canada. Martin stopped Jenny Potter on the deke. Nanna Jansson shot wide for Sweden, and star USA defenceman Angela Ruggiero got two cracks to score. She flubbed the first, but referee Joy Tottman ruled that Martin moved out of her crease before Tottman blew her whistle to start the shot. Krissy Wendell tried to

USA's Kristin King bangs in the loose puck to give her team a 1-0 lead midway through the first period.

Sweden's Pernilla Winberg celebrates with teammates after scoring in the shootout.

deke Martin much like Jansson, and her failure opened the door for the heroics of Winberg and Rooth.

"They had everything to lose and we had everything to gain," said Joa Elfsberg. "The Russians played well against us and we won today, so the games are getting closer and closer. This is a huge step for women's hockey."

The Americans took a 1-0 lead midway through the first when Julie Chu's centre point blast hit Martin's right post and Kristin King pushed the rebound over the goal line.

The Americans went up 2-0 at 1:04 of the second period when Kelly Stephens redirected Lyndsay Wall's shot from the blueline through Martin's legs. The Swedes got back into it at 6:17 when Rooth scored with her back to the net, spinning and firing a backhand while being checked.

Improbably, the Swedes tied the game while playing short-handed when Lyndsay Wall lost the puck to Erika Holst behind the goal line. Holst centered it to Rooth, who got it up over Gunn's glove.

The Swedes took five straight minor penalties in the second, including a lengthy five-on-three, but their shooters drew blanks and Martin stood large in the Swedish net.

"They played a great game, but we squandered some chances, especially the five-on-three when we couldn't score," USA coach Ben Smith conceded. "We haven't had an easy time of it here in our four games."

"We couldn't put the puck in the net," said Wall. "We've had trouble scoring goals all year."

Russia 6 / Switzerland 2

February 17 • Esposizioni • 1:00 p.m.

While Canada and USA appeared to march toward a gold-medal showdown in their respective semi-finals later today, the bottom four teams played games toward determining which teams finish 5th, 6th, 7th, and 8th. By defeating Switzerland this afternoon 6-2, the Russians earned one spot in the 5th-place game on February 20th. This might have been considered a surprising result before the tournament began, but the Russians have played surprisingly well here in Turin.

Teams exchanged goals in the first period, but in the second the Russians exploded for four scores. Larisa Mishina's second goal of the period, the team's fourth, also chased Patricia Elsmore-Sautter from the Swiss net. Kathrin Lehmann scored soon after to draw the team within two, but the Russians remained in control of the game.

Alexandra Kapustina added a power-play goal in the third to complete the scoring.

Germany 5 / Italy 2

February 17 • Esposizioni • 6:30 p.m.

Germany defeated Italy 5-2 in the other placement game before 2,750 fans at the Esposizioni. Refereed by Russian Arina Ustinova, it featured 19 minor penalties, eleven of which were incurred by the winners.

The Germans jumped out to a quick 2-0 lead before the game was six minutes old, but two goals 41 seconds apart by Italy's Maria Michaela Leitner evened the score. She led all players with seven shots in the game. However, Nikola Holmes put Germany back on top for good just 48 seconds later.

The Italians hung tight through the second period, but goals by Maritta Becker (her second of the game) and Nina Ritter salted the German victory in the third period. The Italians scored two goals for the first time at these Olympics, but they remained winless (0-4-0).

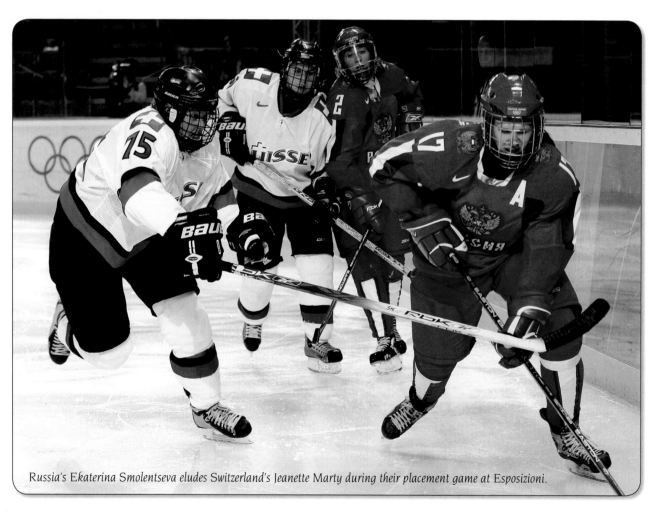

Russia's Ekaterina Smolentseva eludes Switzerland's Jeanette Marty during their placement game at Esposizioni.

Switzerland 2 / Canada 0

February 18 • Esposizioni • 3:30 p.m.

The coach, Ralph Krueger, is a Canadian, from Winnipeg, and the player who scored the only two goals, Paul Di Pietro, is a former NHLer and holder of a Canadian passport. Yet on this day, they conspired with Swiss goalie Martin Gerber to post another extraordinary result at these Olympics, this time a 2-0 Swiss victory over Canada.

"It feels great," said Di Pietro. "There are probably a lot of people back home watching. It's great to compete against the best in the world. You have to enjoy every moment."

Despite David Aebischer's fantastic performance versus the Czech Republic, Krueger decided to go back to Gerber, who had started the team's first game, a 5-0 loss to the Finns. Gerber made a genius of his coach as he stopped all 49 shots he faced, including 24 in the third when the Swiss had exactly one shot on Brodeur and successfully held their lead through defensive work.

"We believed anything was possible tonight, and we never stopped believing," said Krueger.

That possibility was aided by Canada's inept power play which had eleven power-play chances and scored not once. "They're aggressive and they forecheck hard,"

Joe Thornton and the rest of the Canadian team were checked into the ice by the Swiss this day.

GAME SUMMARY

First Period

1 Switzerland, Di Pietro (*Della Rossa*)   18:19

penalties: Nash (Can) 1:00, Blindenbacher (Sui) 1:37, Seger (Sui—minor, misconduct) 2:29, Bertuzzi (Can) & Streit (Sui) 3:43, Streit (Sui) 6:16, Forster (Sui) 9:44, Pluss (Sui) 13:06

Second Period

2 Switzerland, Di Pietro (*Bezina, Streit*)   8:47

penalties: Lemm (Sui) 1:46, Doan (Can) 3:57, Heatley (Can) 6:46, Foote (Can) 7:55, Pronger (Can) 8:37, Forster (Sui) 14:31, Richards (Can) 17:24, Lemm (Sui) 18:11

Third Period

No Scoring

penalties: Pluss (Sui) 2:54, Bertuzzi (Can) 3:12, Lecavalier (Can—minor, misconduct) 8:27, Vauclair (Sui) 11:52, Pluss (Sui—double minor) 13:49, Pronger (Can) 14:58, Streit (Sui) 18:00, Iginla (Can) 18:07, Nash (Can) 19:00, Della Rossa (Sui) 19:20, Vauclair (Sui) 19:59

In Goal

Canada	Brodeur
Switzerland	Gerber

Shots on Goal

Canada	12	13	24	**49**
Switzerland	6	11	1	**18**

Referee	Viacheslav Bulanov (RUS)
Linesmen	Miroslav Halecky (SVK)
	Kevin Redding (USA)
Attendance	4,769

said Pronger. "They're in your face, limiting your time and space. They're a hard team to play against. At times we tried to get a little bit too cute, and they got some momentum from that. We just weren't able to score."

Although Gerber had a great game, most of the shots he faced were from the periphery thanks to amazing team defence. The first period set the tone for the game. Canada had six power plays to one

for the Swiss, and the highlight came on a four-on-three during which Gerber made fine saves on shots from defenceman Chris Pronger and forward Brad Richards.

The Swiss opened the scoring late in the period. Patric Della Rossa got the puck behind Brodeur's goal and pushed a nice pass out to Di Pietro in the slot. He fired quickly before the goalie could react, and the Swiss had their fans screaming with joy.

"I just went to the net, and I got lucky to get it in," said Di Pietro, the only player on the Swiss team that still uses a wooden stick.

La Suisse got a five-on-three opportunity in the second period to open a 2-0 lead. Defenceman Mark Streit, erstwhile part-timer for the Montreal Canadiens, took a shot from the point that hit Robyn Regehr's skate in front. The puck landed fortuitously on Di Pietro's

Goal or save? Gerber's great glove grab was ruled a save after a lengthy video review procedure.

Swiss-Canadian hero Paul Di Pietro shakes hands with the man he beat twice, Canadian goalie Martin Brodeur.

stick, and for the second time in the game he made no mistake with his close-in shot.

Canada scored twice in the second, but neither goal counted. On the first, Todd Bertuzzi knocked in a rebound, but referee Viacheslav Bulanov ruled the Canadian was in the crease.

The second play was far more contentious. Rick Nash took a shot that Gerber caught in his glove while Canada was on another power play. Gerber slid from one post to the other to make the spectacular save, but the Canadians said that Gerber's glove was in the net as he caught the puck. Bulanov went to video review, and after perhaps the lengthiest discussion in video-review history it was ruled that the puck could not conclusively be said to have crossed the goal line.

In the third, the Swiss made no attempt to penetrate the Canadian end or do anything beyond dumping the puck out of their end and checking their man closely. And, although they spent most of the period in their end, Canada could not get into position for point-blank, dangerous shots. Perhaps their best opportunity came on a five-on-three after Joe Sakic was high sticked. Martin Pluss's stick opened a sizeable, and bloody, cut on the captain's cheek, but Pronger then took a lazy slashing penalty to kill that chance and the Canadians couldn't capitalize on the single man advantage.

This was the first victory for the Swiss against Canada in Olympic and World Championship history dating back to 1924. That year, in their first meeting, Canada won 33-0. ♣

Russia 1 / Khazakhstan 0

February 18 • Esposizioni • 11:30 a.m.

Kazakhstan goalie Vitali Yeremeyev stopped 49 of 50 shots he faced against the Russians, but the one shot that got past him, by Alexander Kharitonov midway through the game, proved to be the difference. Evgeni Nabokov got the shutout for the Russians by turning aside 24 shots.

"Yeremeyev was wonderful," said Russian head coach Vladimir Krikunov. "I am satisfied with his play because he plays for my team [Dynamo Moscow] in Russia, and it looks like he's getting ready for the playoffs."

The Kazakhs began the game with inspiration, and with two losses to their credit so far, they knew they needed a point or two if they were to have any chance to advance in the tough Group B which also included Sweden, Slovakia, USA, Russia, and Latvia.

The game was chippy and without much flow as the lesser-skilled Kazakhs tried to slow down the speedy Russians by any means possible. It wasn't until midway through the second that Russia broke through for the game's first, and only, goal.

Kharitonov picked up a loose puck behind the net, and on the wraparound he managed to squeeze it between the post and Yeremeyev's pad. Yeremeyev was sharp in stopping another Kharitonov shot a few minutes later during a five-on-three, and although the Russians held the edge in play and puck possession they couldn't score a second goal.

"We've got to find a way to score more goals," said Nabokov. "If we want to go far, we have to play a complete game."

Teammate Darius Kasparaitis took the opposite approach in analyzing the result. "There are a lot of teams that can score," he explained, "but we have to play defense. Especially in a game like this, we have to have patience and try to win 1-0 or 2-0. It doesn't matter."

Alexander Kharitonov skates by the Russian bench after scoring the game's only goal.

Tony Iob celebrates Italy's second goal to give the team a 2-1 lead.

Italy 3 / Germany 3

February 18 • Palasport • 1:00 p.m.

Italy earned its first point of the tournament with a 3-3 tie against the Germans. Although the bottom line looked impressive, they had three leads and lost each one, the last with just over a minute left in the game.

Perhaps buoyed by the knowledge that anything can happen, or by the noisy Italian crowd, the Italians came out skating with confidence and were rewarded early. John Parco took the puck from the corner where teammate Tony Iob had been cycling it. He came right out in front and tucked the puck in the far side past a surprised Olaf Kolzig to give the Italians a 1-0 lead just 2:03 into the game.

The Germans managed to poke the puck over the goal line in the second when Tino Boos, like Parco in the first, came out from behind the net and tried to stuff the puck in. Jason Muzzatti stood his ground, but the biscuit landed on the stick of Tomas Martinec and he lifted it over the fallen goalie to tie the game at 6:21

In the third, Daniel Kruetzer, turned the puck over while skating lazily out of his end. He was pokechecked by Parco, and Parco backhanded a pass to Iob in the slot for the go-ahead goal.

The Germans came right back, though, and tied the game again, at 7:16, when the culprit Kruetzer made a nice little pass to Sven Felski in the slot. His low shot beat Muzzatti cleanly.

The Italians were served with what they felt was an undeserved penalty at 16:51 when Parco was sent off for tripping. However, they scored what they thought was the game winner while playing short-handed. Christian Borgatello came in on a two-on-one with Giorgio de Bettin, and de Bettin put a perfect pass across the slot which Borgatello drove beautifully to the top corner for the go-ahead goal.

The lead lasted only a few seconds. German coach Uwe Krupp called a time out and then lifted Kolzig, and the Germans got the puck deep into the Italian end. Marcel Goc got the puck in the slot. He faked a shot, moved around the defenceman, and shot again, beating Muzzatti to the stick side for the game's final goal just 15 seconds after Borgatello's.

February 18 • Palasport • 5:00 p.m.

It took all of 14:20 for Peter Forsberg to make his first impression for Sweden at the 2006 Olympics, an impression that helped take his team to an easy 6-1 victory over Latvia this afternoon at Palasport. He collected the puck near centre, skated down the left side and drove hard to the net. His shot was stopped by Latvian goalie Sergejs Naumovs, but the rebound landed right on the stick of Samuel Pahlsson and he drilled the puck into the open net. Foppa was back, and Sweden had atoned for a miserable showing against Russia two nights earlier.

"I felt good out there tonight," Forsberg said after coming off the ice. "It was good to start with a bit of an easier opponent for my first game, but I felt fine."

Forsberg still feels he has a bit of a ways to go before declaring himself 100% fit, though. "It's going to take a while before I'm in game shape, but I hope to get there by the quarterfinals."

Tre Kronor was in control from the outset, and early in the second they broke the game open with four unanswered goals. They got their second goal when Nicklas Lidstrom rifled a seeing-eye point shot on the power play through a screen of players in front and past Naumovs. Three minutes later, they struck on the power play again, this time Daniel Alfredsson finishing a pass from Kenny Jonsson. The fourth came on a lovely feed from Forsberg to Axelsson to the back door of the beleaguered goalie Naumovs. Number five came on a great Zetterberg backhand with Naumovs way out of position. Still, coach Leonids Beresnevs kept his goalie in the net when it was clear Naumovs was having an off day.

In the third, Mats Sundin tried his patented wraparound on the backhand, and Alfredsson was in front to get the loose puck and stick it in the corner to make it 6-0. Maris Ziedins scored for Latvia when the game was long out of reach.

Peter Forsberg was all smiles in his return to the Sweden lineup against Latvia.

Derian Hatcher clears the puck from harm's way as goalie Rick DiPietro scrambles to his feet.

Slovakia 2 / USA 1

February 18 • Esposizioni • 8:00 p.m.

Peter Bondra scored the go-ahead goal in the third period and Slovakia held on to beat USA 2-1 and maintain a perfect record (3-0-0). The Americans are now 1-1-1.

"I think it was a great game, a very close game," Slovakia's Pavol Demitra said. "All our four lines contributed something, and we played great defensively. We waited for the right breaks, and we got two of them. There was a great atmosphere too, with a lot of our fans and a lot of U.S. fans too."

The game was close and exciting from start to finish, starting with great rushes by Mike Modano and Marian Gaborik, two of the fastest skaters in the world. The tempo they helped establish held up for the rest of the game, even though they didn't score on all of their end-to-end rushes.

Just past the midway mark of the period, Gaborik drilled a shot off the post, and before the end of the period the U.S. had a great chance when a scramble in front saw several players try to bang home the loose puck. Brian Gionta trapped goalie Peter Budaj out of the crease on another chance, but as he shot into the open net defenceman Zdeno Chara slid to block the shot and save a sure goal.

Slovakia opened the scoring at 14:20 of the second on the power play. Pavol Demitra hit Marian Hossa with a pass down the right side, and Hossa's quick wrist shot fooled Rick DiPietro and slipped between his legs.

Rolston tied the game on an American man advantage four minutes later when he blew a wicked slapshot past Budaj into the top corner.

The winning goal was the result of a series of little errors around the American goal. Chris Chelios tried to check Miroslav Satan behind the American goal, but he fell awkwardly. In that moment, Satan made a quick pass in the slot to Bondra, who one-timed a low shot past DiPietro while four American players converged on him but failed to prevent him from shooting.

"That was a perfect pass," said Bondra. "I couldn't do anything else but shoot the puck at the net."

Finland 4 / Czech Republic 2

February 18 • Palasport • 9:00 p.m.

The Finns and Czechs hooked up for a game that had a little bit of everything--great goals, great saves, and high emotions as a result of a hit from behind that left Jaromir Jagr bloodied and Jarkku Ruutu banished from the game. The result was a hard-fought 4-2 Finland victory.

"He suffered no concussion", said Czech coach Alois Hadamczik, who also said that the hit on Jagr overshadowed an otherwise exciting game. "He will play tomorrow if he feels well enough."

The Czechs scored the opening goal on a power play. Marek Zidlicky moved in from the right point and took a pass, but instead of blasting away he faked the shot, walked around the sprawling forward who had tried to block it, and then drilled a low shot to Antero Niittymaki's far side that caught the corner.

The Finns tied the game at 14:14 when they gained control of the puck in their own end just as Saku Koivu came out of the penalty box. Ville Peltonen made the long outlet pass as Koivu streaked up the wing, and Olli Jokinen blazed through the middle. Koivu waited, and at the perfect moment that Jokinen arrived in the slot fed him a beautiful pass. Jokinen simply redirected the puck into the open side.

All hell broke loose in the second period. Jagr was in the Finnish corner with the puck, fighting for possession with a Finn. Jarkko Ruutu saw Jagr was vulnerable, lined him up, and hit him viciously from behind. Jagr fell to the ice in a pool of blood, and Martin Straka jumped Ruutu, who received a five-minute major and match penalty for attempt to injure.

In the end, it was the Finns who got the next goal, on a power play at that. It came off a point shot that the goalie stopped but couldn't control. The puck squirted free of Vokoun's pads, and Jere Lehtinen banged in the rebound at 15:02.

Zidlicky tied the game for the Czechs on a five-on-three when he blasted a shot by a helpless Niittymaki from the high slot.

Teemu Selanne got the Finns back in front just 30 seconds after the start of the third. His weak shot in front was blocked, but the puck came back to him and his high second shot handcuffed Vokoun and dribbled into the net. Lehtinen rounded out the scoring with his second of the game.

Saku Koivu opens the scoring in the first period, beating Tomas Vokoun with a one-timer.

Paul Di Pietro Beats Canada

A native of Sault Ste. Marie, Paul Di Pietro played junior hockey for his hometown Wolves and was drafted 102nd overall by the Montreal Canadiens in 1990. Like most any NHL player, he started in the minors, playing for Fredericton for a year and a half before being called up to the big team in 1991-92.

The highlight of his career came in '92-'93 when he played the year with the team which went on to win the Stanley Cup, defeating Wayne Gretzky and Los Angeles. It was Montreal's last Cup to date.

Di Pietro played the better part of three years with the Canadiens before being traded to Toronto, but after just a few games with the Leafs in 1994-95 he was back to the minors.

His final NHL time came with Los Angeles in '96-'97, and the year after, with few decent offers on the table, he signed with Kassel in Germany. The next year he moved on to Ambri-Piotta in Switzerland, and he has been playing in that country ever since. Now 35, he played 2005-06 with Zug.

As a result of his extended stay in Switzerland he became a Swiss player and citizen and now holds two passports. This made him eligible for international play, and he made his debut with La Suisse at the 2005 World Championship where he scored one goal in seven games. His appearance in Torino marked his first Olympics, and the highlight of the tournament came when he scored twice to defeat Canada 2-0 during the round-robin play.

Paul Di Pietro celebrates his first of two goals against Canada in Switzerland's stunning 2-0 victory.

Finland 2 / Canada 0

February 19 • Esposizioni • 9:00 p.m.

There was something in the air at the Torino Esposizioni where two of the heavy hitters, Canada and Finland, played a big-time hockey game. But for the second straight game, Canada came out on the short end, and for the fourth straight game the Finns won. The score was 2-0, and it was made enjoyable all the more because it was refereed to utter perfection by Vladimir Sindler.

Canada, stocked with offensive talent, has now played 120 minutes (six periods) without scoring a goal. The team also lost to Switzerland 2-0 yesterday. The last time the team was shut out in consecutive games was February 17/19, 1984.

Right from the drop of the puck it was clear that Canadian goalie Roberto Luongo had brought his A-game to the rink. He stopped Teemu Selanne as the speedy Finn drove a shot while barreling down the right wing. In truth, Luongo kept the game scoreless through the first half of the period with his play, notably on a five-on-three for Finland.

Despite those two penalties, referee Vladimir Sindler let the players play, and tonight that meant play physically. Hard hitting and finishing checks were the order of the night, and nobody was the worse for it.

Finland opened the scoring when tiny captain Saku Koivu stripped 6'6" defenceman Chris Pronger of the puck behind the Canadian goal. Koivu tossed the puck in the slot, and Teemu Selanne made no mistake with his one-timer at 11:14. Shots on goal to that point were 11-2 for the Finns.

They added to their lead at 11:02 courtesy of one of many faceoff wins in the Canada zone. Kimmo Timonen took a point shot that drifted over

GAME SUMMARY

First Period

1	Finland, Selanne (*Koivu*)	11:14
2	Finland, Kapanen (*Nieminen, Timonen*)	15:02

penalties: Regehr (Can) 5:11, Pronger (Can) 6:53, Nash (Can) 15:39

Second Period

No Scoring

penalties: Lydman (Fin) 2:13, Gagne (Can) 3:50, Foote (Can) 6:29

Third Period

No Scoring

penalties: Hagman (Fin) 10:49, Pronger (Can) 13:29, Laaksonen (Fin) 17:37

In Goal

Finland	Niittymaki
Canada	Luongo

Shots on Goal

Finland	14	11	5	**30**
Canada	5	12	7	**24**

Referee	Vladimir Sindler (CZE)
Linesmen	Milan Masik (SVK)
	Thor Eric Nelson (USA)
Attendance	4,420

Finland's Saku Koivu (left) lines up for a faceoff with Canada's Brad Richards.

Goalie Antero Niittymaki makes the save while Canada's Todd Bertuzzi crashes the net.

the net, but it hit the glass and came right back into the slot, past Luongo's stick and over Rob Blake's as well. Niko Kapanen wristed the puck into the empty side of the net.

"We didn't get off to the start we wanted," Ryan Smyth admitted. "But we're not going to panic. We were in a similar position in Salt Lake, and this is a great team we have here. We have high expectations."

Canada took its wake-up meds during the first intermission and came out with a greater sense of urgency in the second. The team picked up the pace considerably when Simon Gagne came out of the penalty box and tore down the left wing for a good shot on goal. The next couple of minutes were played exclusively in the Finnish end, and Antero Niittymaki had to have his wits about him in the Finnish net. He put together a string of fine saves, including on a shot in the slot from Rick Nash, a point blast from Bryan McCabe, and a chance in front by Brad Richards.

The Finns came to life, storming Luongo with fresh energy at the thought of a Canadian goal, and this time it was the Canadian goalie who came up big—with the help of Lady Luck. Luongo made one partial-glove save only to have the puck land fortuitously on the top of the net.

The save of the period, though, went to Niittymaki who robbed Nash cold on a clear-cut breakaway to keep the score 2-0.

"I could see there were a couple of my teammates chasing him [Nash]," Niittymaki explained, "so I knew he was going to shoot. I just tried to block as much of the net as possible."

Canada continued to press in the third, and Niittymaki was there again to make a nice save on a back-door shot from Martin St. Louis. He robbed Joe Thornton from five feet out and frustrated the Canadians who hadn't scored since the final minute of their game against Germany last week.

When the game was over, the Finns were full marks for the win, even if Canada did outplay them for the final two periods.

"We didn't give up many three-on-twos and two-on-ones," Timonen noted. "That was important to us."

"We have to simplify our game," Canadian defenceman Adam Foote said. "We need to play more direct hockey. Stops and starts. There's pressure on us, for sure, but right now we have to forget about that."

Canada's efforts to get back into the win column don't get any easier as it plays the Czech Republic on Tuesday. The Finns try to remain perfect when they finish against Germany that day. ☘

Finland was the only team to celebrate goals this night, shutting out Canada, 2-0.

Paul Di Pietro celebrates his go-ahead goal against goalie Olaf Kolzig and the Germans.

Germany 2 / Switzerland 2

February 19 • Palasport • 12:00 p.m.

Germany and Switzerland played to a 2-2 tie, improving the Swiss record to 2-1-1 while the Germans were still winless (0-2-2).

"The game was hard-fought and close," said German coach Uwe Krupp. "In the third period I thought we outplayed the Swiss. They appeared a little tired to me."

Swiss coach Ralph Krueger continued alternating his goalies, starting David Aebischer 24 hours after Martin Gerber had stopped 49 shots in a 2-0 shutout win over Canada. The rest of the team was naturally a little flat after that huge win and didn't play as well as it had against the Canadians. Nonetheless, the tie gives them a place in the quarter-finals.

The Germans scored the opening goal 2:20 into the second period when Sven Felski scooped a rebound off a Christian Ehrhoff screen shot that Aebischer couldn't control.

The Swiss evened the score five minutes later thanks to some good work from Patrick Fischer. He dashed through the middle and was stopped by Kolzig on the initial shot, but Fischer went behind the net to get the puck and fired it out front to Flavien Conne who popped it home.

Paul Di Pietro, yesterday's two-goal hero, scored again today near the end of the second when he walked out from the corner and took a bad-angle shot that bounced off the stick of German defenceman Marcel Goc and past Kolzig.

The Germans scored the tying goal midway through the final period when Tino Boos had several whacks at a loose puck and the Swiss defencemne failed to check him.

Russia 9 / Latvia 2

February 19 • Esposizioni • 1:00 p.m.

Ilya Kovalchuk scored his first four goals of these Olympics in the first two periods of today's game at Esposizioni, leading Russia to a 9-2 romp over Latvia.

Ilya Kovalchuk scored half his team's eight goals in an easy 9-2 win over Latvia.

"We wanted to come out strong today because we thought the game against Kazakhstan would be easy and it wasn't," Kovalchuk noted. "But I still don't think we have played our best hockey yet."

The Russians got on the board first at 7:26 after prolonged puck possession in the Latvian end. Ilya Kovalchuk set the red goal light ablaze when he went around the net, stopped, and cut back to the near side where he tucked the puck under the scrambling Arturs Irbe.

They upped their lead two minutes later on a five-on-three when Alexander Kharitonov made a great pass across to Maxim Sushinksy who one-timed the puck into the open side at 9:15.

Just 40 seconds later, though, still down a man, the Latvians broke out on a two-on-one and the puck carrier, Aigars Cipruss, took the shot. His low drive to the far side beat goalie Evgeni Nabokov cleanly.

Fine Russian individual efforts secured the team its third goal. Pavel Datsyuk picked the puck up at centre, split the defence with brilliant ease, and just at the crease he pushed the puck to Kovalchuk as Irbe was playing the shooter and Kovalchuk had his second goal of the period by tapping home the soft pass.

"That was the easiest goal, for sure," Kovalchuk said with a smile. "Pavel made a great pass." Kovalchuk completed his hat trick off a faceoff win and a great one-timer.

Viktor Kozlov made it 5-1 when he followed his shot to the net and picked up the rebound. Unchecked, he popped the loose pill behind a splayed Irbe. The game was over; the rout was on. And, Irbe was retired to the bench in favour of Edgars Masalskis.

At 15:16 Kovalchuk made his afternoon special, slapping in a loose puck from the slot to give him four goals and running the score to 6-1. Alexei Yashin, Evgeni Malkin, and Alexander Ovechkin added to the total in the third. Mikelis Redlihs scored a meaningless goal for Latvia near the end to make it 9-2.

Slovakia 2 / Kazakhstan 1

February 19 • Palasport • 4:00 p.m.

Marian Hossa's third-period, go-ahead goal stood as the winner as Slovakia defeated a stubborn Kazakh team that lost its second straight squeaker. Russia beat Kazakhstan just 1-0 the previous night in another surprisingly close game.

"We fulfilled our goal for the game," said Slovak coach Frantisek Hossa. "The Kazakh players played bravely, and they were a hard opponent." Indeed, Slovakia had ten power plays but cashed in only once, fair tribute to the determination of the weaker team despite a lack of pure skill and talent.

"I think we've been practicing the penalty kill for the last four games," said Nikolai Antropov. "We've played almost the equivalent of one game shorthanded. There's nothing you can do about it. You just go out there and defend your net."

From the outset it appeared that the Slovaks were not approaching the game with the same intensity that had made them successful to this point. They paid the price later in the period when Kazakhstan opened the scoring, on a power play at 16:16. Yevgeniy Koreshkov accepted a pass from his brother, Alexandr, in the slot and his one-timer beat Karol Kristan cleanly.

The Kazakhs were poised to carry their slim 1-0 lead into the final period, but the Slovaks tied the game at 19:50 on a power play of their own. Milan Jurcina caught Kolesnik out of position and passed to a wide open Peter Bondra who banged the puck into the open side. It was a frustrating goal for the Kazakhs to give up and gave Slovakia something to build on for the third period.

Indeed, Slovakia scored the eventual game winner at the 8:09 mark. Pavol Demitra flew down the left wing into the corner of the Kazakh end, and while he looked to be passing to Lubomir Visnovsky he instead made a nifty pass to Marian Hossa who made no mistake in close with his shot.

Coach Frantisek Hossa had one fewer players than normal for the final two periods because he entered the name of Josef Stumpel incorrectly on the official lineup. So, after playing the first period, Stumpel had to undress once the error had been discovered.

Referee Danny Kurmann signals Marian Hossa's game-winning goal in the third period.

Sweden 2 / USA 1

February 19 • Esposizioni • 5:00 p.m.

Mikael Samuelsson's third-period goal on the power play provided the margin of victory as Sweden defeated USA 2-1 at Esposizioni. Both teams were playing their fourth game in five days after their trans-Atlantic flight, but Sweden's captain Daniel Alfredsson said he felt no ill effects. "I feel better and better, actually. It's easier playing this schedule than playing that first game after the time difference and jet lag."

The teams went end-to-end looking for the first goal. It finally came after Mats Sundin put the puck back to the point in the USA end. Kenny Jonsson took the shot, but goaltender Rick DiPietro couldn't control the rebound. Alfredsson calmly claimed

the puck, waited for the goalie to go down, and roofed the puck while falling away from the goal at 7:05 for the early lead.

Team USA tied the game at 17:31 on a delayed penalty. Pahlsson took his man down at the blueline and lost his stick in the process, and while his hands were in the air as he pleaded his innocence to referee Dan Marouelli, Craig Conroy took the puck into the corner and passed to Mike Modano in the slot. Modano drilled a shot to the far side that beat Henrik Lundqvist cleanly.

The second started more cautiously until the U.S. was given a five-on-three situation. Lundqvist made several huge saves to weather the storm, and on one sequence, John-Michael Liles lost the puck at the blueline and Axelsson went in alone on DiPietro. He failed to score

the rarest of all goals (two men short) when he deked in too close to the goalie and couldn't get a decent shot away.

Sweden ran into further penalty trouble when two more penalties just seconds apart gave USA another lengthy five-on-three, this one lasting 1:55. Once again, Lundqvist and the penalty killers were outstanding.

"The key to the game was killing those five-on-threes," Alfredsson noted. "The penalty kill was great and Lundqvist was great in goal."

The USA's Mike Modano agreed. "We have to score in those situations. We just didn't bury the puck."

Ironically, Sweden got the winning goal on an early power play in the third when Alfredsson's shot squeezed through the pads of DiPietro and lay in the crease for Mikael Samuelsson to bang home.

The line of captain Mats Sundin-Mikael Samuelsson (#33), and Daniel Alfredsson (#11) celebrate their first-period goal.

Action gets heavy around the Italian net as goalie Jason Muzzatti loses the puck for a moment during Italy's 4-1 loss to the Czechs.

Czech Republic 4 / Italy 1

February 19 • Palasport • 8:00 p.m.

Although Jaromir Jagr was still a bit shaken up after the dirty hit the previous day from Finland's Jarkku Ruutu, he started for the Czechs in their routine 4-1 win over Italy. But, once the game's outcome was clear, Jagr went to the dressing room early and called it a night. Vaclav Prospal had a hat trick for the winning side.

"We felt a little bit of pressure that we had to win, but we were still pretty confident," said Milan Hejduk. "We're a better team and we should win a game like this. But the way we're playing right now, it's not the best."

The Czechs got that all-important first goal at 12:57 of the opening period thanks to some nice puck movement in the Italian end. David Vyborny made a nice pass to Tomas Kaberle at the point, and his shot was stopped by goalie Gunther Hell. Milan Hejduk was right there, however, to put the rebound into the net.

Less than two minutes later, Prospal got his first of the night on a great play behind Italy's goal. He held the puck for what seemed like ages, faking to come out in front one side, then the other, until finally he went the way Hell was not expecting and tucked it in for a 2-0 Czech lead.

The Czechs took a conclusive 3-0 lead at 8:36 when Prospal tracked down a too-long pass from Martin Straka. Jason Muzzatti, who had replaced Hell a short time earlier in the Italian net, tried to get to the puck first but lost the race. The result was an easy empty-netter for Prospal.

Italy's only consolation was in ruining Tomas Vokoun's shutout with a goal at 17:53. John Parco snapped home a Giorgio de Bettin pass on a two-on-one. Prospal closed out the scoring with an empty-net goal at 18:40, Muzzatti on the bench in a desperate attempt by the Italians to score again.

USA 4 / Finland 0

February 20 • Palasport • 4:30 p.m.

This wasn't how it was supposed to turn out for USA, but this is how it did. A 4-0 workout against Finland gave the Americans a bronze medal. They won gold in 1998 and silver in 2002. Katie King had a hat trick to finish with six goals in the tournament. After the game, she announced her retirement.

"For us, this was the gold medal game," she said. "We wanted to win tonight. It was tough the last few days to get ready for the game, but we played with pride."

"We're very disappointed," said Finland's Mari Pehkonen about the result. "We were ready physically and emotionally to win. We didn't have the start that we wanted to. The first period decided everything."

American goalie Chanda Gunn needed to make just 14 saves for the shutout. Noora Raty of Finland was replaced by Maija Hassinen early in the second period.

The U.S. got the early jump in the game and scored just 2:32 into the game when Julie Chu's point shot was redirected in front by Kelly Stephens.

At 8:09, Katie King got her first of the night when she sped down the right wing and drove hard to the net. She outwaited Raty and flipped the puck over the sprawling goalie and into the net to make it 2-0.

Action heats up in front of Finnish goalie Noora Raty.

Three minutes later, King took a pass from Jenny Potter in full flight coming up ice and used her speed to create a breakaway. She made a great shot to the top corner over Raty's stick side to give the Americans a cushion they could feel confident with.

King finished her natural hat trick at 1:44 of the second. She ripped a high shot over Raty's shoulder again after taking a nice feed form Chu. At this point, coach Hannu Saintila made the goalie change.

The rest of the game was played at a slower tempo as the Americans were content to win by this score and the Finns were unable to mount a serious charge or capitalize on the few scoring chances they had. The result was a medal victory for USA, albeit a bronze.

Finland's players and coaches look on during their bronze-medal game against USA.

American Krissy Wendell (left) shakes hands with Satu Kiipeli after USA took the bronze medal with a 4-0 win over Finland.

February 20 • Esposizioni • 1:00 p.m.
7th Place Game

A balanced attack from the Swiss produced a lop-sided win in today's placement game to the tune of 11-0 at Italy's expense. The result means that the Swiss finish the Olympics in seventh place and the Italians eighth place. Five players had two goals apiece for Switzerland--Laura Ruhnke, Stephanie Marty, Julie Marty, Daniella Diaz, and Kathrin Lehmann. Lehmann also had two assists. Christine Meier had the other goal.

The Swiss scored four goals in the first period, chasing Debora Montanari from the net. Luana Frasnelli started the second period for Italy and went the rest of the way. The host nation finished the tournament after losing all five of its games by an aggregate score of 48-3. Nonetheless, once the Swiss team left the ice, the Italians waved to the fans and received a standing ovation in honour of their participation at this year's Olympics.

Today's win was the first for the Swiss here in Turin.

February 20 • Esposizioni • 5:00 p.m.
5th Place Game

Germany and Russia played 70 minutes of scoreless hockey before Germany decided the game with two penalty shots in the shootout, following a 10-minute overtime period. Maritta Becker and Nikola Holmes were the only successful shooters. German goaltender Jennifer Harss stopped four Russian shooters.

Germany finished fifth in the Olympic tournament, the same place the team had in the IIHF World Championship last year. It was the German women's best placing in the Olympics. They finished 6th in Salt Lake City 2002.

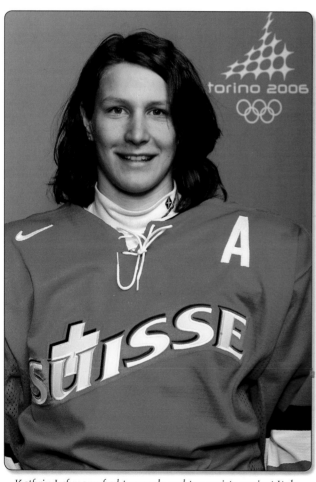

Kathrin Lehmann had two goals and two assists against Italy.

Maritta Becker scored the winner in the shootout for Germany.

Canada 4 / Sweden 1

February 20 • Palasport • 8:30 p.m.

There was to be no Swedish Mirakel at the expense of 2002 gold medalists Canada tonight at Palasport. Despite the amazing semi-final win by the Swedes over USA, they were no match for a team that scores far more goals than it gives up shots by the opposition. Tonight, the score was 4-1. The girls of Canada were golden again. Although they had all sorts of firepower, it was their play inside their own blueline that won this championship.

It was a nervous start for both teams, but Gillian Apps got rid of the butterflies just 3:15 from the opening faceoff when she skated in a large arc through the Swedish slot all the while on her backhand and then let go a simple shot along the ice that fooled goalie Kim Martin. It was Apps's 7th goal of the tournament, and it was a shot Martin should have saved, especially in light of her brilliant semi-final performance.

The game settled back into a cautious one, but Sweden, for all their efforts, could not establish puck possession in the Canadian end for any length of time, so good was the Canadian team defence. Charline Labonte was the starter for Canada, but the net could have been empty so

Goalie Charline Labonte leaps in the air at the final horn as Canada wins gold.

GAME SUMMARY

First Period
1. Canada, Apps (*Wickenheiser*) — 3:15
2. Canada, Ouellette (*Hefford, Botterill*) — 12:13

penalties: Jansson (Swe) 3:39, Asserholt (Swe) 13:18, Apps (Can) 15:14

Second Period
3. Canada, Piper (*Wickenheiser, Pounder*) — 8:58
4. Canada, Hefford (*Botterill, Vaillancourt*) — 10:27

penalties: Swe (*too many players*) 11:14, Sostorics (Can) 15:37

Third Period
5. Sweden, Andersson (*Holst, Rooth*) — 5:24

penalties: Ouellette (Can) 4:29, Wickenheiser (Can) 18:10, Ouellette (Can) 20:00

In Goal

Canada	Labonte
Sweden	Martin

Shots on Goal

Canada	11	11	4	**26**
Sweden	2	3	3	**8**

Referee	Anu Hirvonen (FIN)
Linesmen	Klara Quagliato (CZE)
	Johanna Suban (FIN)
Attendance	6,664

strong were the five players in front of her. It wasn't so much that Canada had a huge lead as much as it was that any lead was insurmountable.

With a more controlled pace, the Canadians slowly but surely took over. They upped their lead at 12:13 on a gorgeous pass by Jennifer Botterill to Caroline Ouellette. Botterill skated down the left side and waited for Ouellette to go to the net. Despite being covered by Jenny Lindqvist, Ouellette got her stick on the puck and flicked it by Martin.

Shots in the first were 11-2 for Canada. It marked one of the few times in the tournament that the opposition had as many shots as Canada had goals in a period.

Canada almost increased the lead to 3-0 at the start of the second when Apps made a lovely drop pass to Wickenheiser who went in alone only to be stoned by Martin. Wickenheiser got her revenge a few minutes later when she carried the puck from centre in and around the Swedish goal and fed Cherie Piper in the slot. Piper made no mistake with her wrist shot, and that more or less solidified the game. Canada, after all, had given up one goal in international competition since 2004 (that to Sweden in the round robin).

Another beautiful pass Botterill to Hefford less than two minutes later made clear the gold medal was heading back to Canada.

The Swedes made things marginally interesting early in the third when they scored on a power play. Gunilla Andersson blasted a point shot that eluded the screened Labonte on the short side to make it 4-1. That's as close as they got.

Wickenheiser led the women's side of the Olympics with 17 points and was named tournament MVP just as she was in 2002. The Directorate Awards went to Wickenheiser as Best Forward, Angela Ruggiero as Best Defenceman, and Kim Martin as Best Goalie. The media All-Stars had Martin in goal, Ruggiero and Carla MacLeod (CAN) on defence, and Wickenheiser, Apps, and Rooth as the forwards. ♣

Cherie Piper celebrates a Canadian goal as Swedish goalie Kim Martin slumps in despair.

(l. to r.) Jayna Hefford, Cassie Campbell, and Vicky Sunohara show off their gold medals.

The Canadians celebrate one of their four goals on a gold medal night.

Gold Medal Notes and Quotes

"2010 might be my last Olympics, but I'll be 31 then, and that's not really old, I don't think. It's just a matter of the other things you want to do in your life. I think to play and finish in Vancouver would be fabulous. What am I going to do next? I'm going to take my son to Disney World. That's a true story! I'll just take a couple of months off. It's been a lot of years for me, going strong. It's time to enjoy being a mom and taking my son to school and being at home for a change."

Hayley Wickenheiser, Canada

"I'm so proud of my players and staff. From the day after we lost the World Championships, we were all committed to winning gold here. Tonight was our 52nd game of the year. We played 46 games leading up to the Olympics. This allowed us to have some sort of real hockey season, and I think that was very important for our team."

Melody Davidson, Canadian Head Coach

Hayley Wickenheiser (left, with son) and Cassie Campbell watch Canada's flag rise into the air of Palasport as O Canada *is played.*

"With 45 seconds left in the game, I realized we were going to be gold medalists. It was great to have my parents in the crowd. They've been so supportive. Growing up, they let me play numerous sports, which helped develop all my skills. If I had a 7 a.m. or late night practice, they'd take me there and they'd sit and watch. Without parents as supportive as them, I would never be here."

Katie Weatherston, Canada

"This year, we were involved with a men's midget AAA league in Calgary, and that helped us tremendously because we were able to play at that level. They raised our level and forced us to keep our heads up and pass the puck harder and all those things. We had a lot of games in our schedule, and we could just see the improvement as we went along."

Cheryl Pounder, Canada

"I was just so happy to get the start in goal. All this work over the last five years has paid off, when I've been sitting in the stands so many nights."

Charline Labonte, Canada

Canada 3 / Czech Republic 2

February 21 • Palasport • 4:30 p.m.

Canada's 3-2 victory over the Czechs tonight placed the team in third in Group A standings, setting up a quarter-finals date with its greatest international adversary—Russia. It wasn't the prettiest win, but at a time when Canada needed to score some goals, get a win, and lift its spirits, any kind of win will do. Best of all, goalie Martin Brodeur was the star for the Canadians, stopping 31 of 33 shots.

"Marty played well, no doubt about it," said Czech forward Martin Rucinsky. "We put a lot of shots on him and he stopped them all."

Canada built a 3-0 lead after the first period and then sat back and tried to protect the lead. It was a great defensive effort, but only barely. The Czechs dominated the final 40 minutes and did everything but put the tying shot past Brodeur.

"When they're dictating the play, what you want to do is get all five guys in the zone," said Rob Blake. "I think we did a good job of that. These are skilled players, and that's the best way to handle them."

GAME SUMMARY

First Period

1	Canada, Richards (*Iginla, Pronger*)	7:37
2	Canada, St. Louis (*Lecavalier, Blake*)	11:19
3	Canada, Pronger (*Thornton*)	19:24

penalties: F. Kaberle (Cze) 10:45, Lang (Cze) 14:10

Second Period

4	Czech Republic, Kubina (*Jagr, Rucinsky*)	13:46

penalties: Igina (Can) 12:31, Blake (Can) 13:32, McCabe (Can) 17:58

Third Period

5	Czech Republic, Cajanek (T. *Kaberle, Hemsky*)	2:41

penalties: McCabe (Can) 10:26

In Goal

Canada	Brodeur
Czech Republic	Vokoun (1st)
	Hnilicka (2nd, 3rd)

Shots on Goal

Canada	8	6	2	**16**
Czech Republic	7	14	12	**33**

Referee	Dan Marouelli (CAN)
Linesmen	Joacim Karlsson (SWE),
	Thor Eric Nelson (USA)
Attendance	9,126

Defenceman Robyn Regehr chases a loose puck while Vaclav Prospal chases Regehr.

Canada got on the scoresheet first by virtue of a lucky goal, which was just what the team needed. Brad Richards skated in over the blueline, and covered by three men with no passing options he fired a quick wrist shot on net. Tomas Vokoun fluffed the shot and it skipped through his legs and into the net. It was the first goal for Canada in more than 128 minutes of play, and the collective relief on the Canadian bench when Richards's shot went in was palpable.

The Canadians went up by two on the power play, again getting a break they never got in the two shutout losses to Switzerland and Finland. Martin St. Louis was stationed right along the goal live to Vokoun's left, and he got a pass and quickly fired it at the net. The puck bounced off the pad of Vokoun and in. Another lucky goal; another sigh of relief; a 2-0 lead.

"The last couple of games we were firing goose eggs, and that's obviously something you don't want to do heading into your elimination game," said Draper. "We needed to find a way to score goals."

The Canadians played with a confidence that comes with a lead, and they were impressive the rest of the period. The Czechs had a couple of good chances, but Brodeur made a nice save on a stuff-in attempt by David Vyborny.

At the other end, the team extended its lead to three goals when a scramble in the slot saw Joe Thornton pass into the slot where Chris Pronger stepped into a slapshot that whizzed by Vokoun at unstoppable speed. Canada skipped into the dressing room up by three and feeling great about the game.

Milan Hnilicka replaced Vokoun in goal to start the second, and five minutes in he proved his worth by stopping St. Louis on a breakaway and again a few minutes later on another chance in close. The Czechs started to play with more authority and desperation, and on a team with that much skill only good things could result. Marek Malik drove a shot that squeaked through Brodeur's pads, but as the puck dribbled to the goal line Bryan McCabe pushed the puck under the fallen Brodeur to nullify a sure goal.

The play of the period went to Brodeur when he made a phenomenal glove save off a Jaromir Jagr. one-timer on a rush with less than eight minutes to go in the period. A few minutes later, though, the Czechs struck when they were given a five-on-three situation. Jagr made a pass to Pavel Kubina in the high slot and his blast eluded Brodeur.

Brodeur made his only mistake of the game early in the third when he flubbed a routine shot from Petr Cajanek. The puck found a space under the goalie's glove arm to make the score 3-2. Despite the renewed efforts by the Czechs to complete the rally, Brodeur stood large in the net the rest of the way. Case in point, on the next shift Cajanek swooped in on goal and faked a shot until Brodeur went down. The player slid the puck toward the wide open side of the net only to have the goalie dive pack, put the paddle down, and make the spectacular stop.

Looking ahead to the quarter-finals, Canada's coach Quinn remarked, "We all know that emotional control is probably a bigger key than actual skill when it comes to games like these. We have guys who have been there before. We've got to be a better team and we will be tomorrow." ✤

Goalie Martin Brodeur kicks out his left pad to make a save.

Kazakhstan 5 / Latvia 2

February 21 • Esposizioni • 11:30 p.m.

It may have been a meaningless game in the Preliminary Round standings, but the Latvian fans who banged drums and chanted "Latvija! Latvija!" all game could have cared less. They had a great time, but their team didn't enjoy the game as much, losing 5-2 to Kazakhstan.

Kazakhstan entered the game in last place in the Group B standings, the Kazakhs having scored a paltry four goals in as many games. That didn't stop them from scoring first, though.

Alexandr Koreshkov took a pass from brother Yevgeniy just inside the Latvian blueline and his routine slapshot beat Sergejs Naumovs to the far side for the early lead. This got the Latvians' attention and they started to play with more purpose.

The Kazakhs responded in kind and produced a solid first period in which they took the play to Latvia. They lost that momentum when Alexey Vassilchenko took a holding penalty and Latvia converted. Well, Kazakhstan converted, actually.

Leonids Tambijevs tried to bang in a loose puck but Artyom Argokov got his stick on the puck first. In attempting to clear the puck, he slapped it right at his own goal and beat Vitaliy Yeremeyev between the legs with the shot. Tambijevs was given credit for the goal nonetheless.

Nikolai Antropov scored the go-ahead goal for Kazakhstan at 15:04 of the second. Yevgeniy Koreshkov fed him a nice pass in the slot and Antropov backhanded the puck through the legs of Naumovs to give the Kazaks a well-deserved 2-1 lead.

A blooper goal for Latvia tied the game 2-2 early in the third. Aigars Cipruss's shot from the point bounced off Kazakhstan's Vassilchenko, took an odd bounce, and ended inside the net.

A Kazakhstan breakout play restored the one-goal lead, and sealed the win as Sergey Alexandrov, with only one man to beat, snapped in the shot. Kazakhstan rolled along after the goal and netted two more goals to close their Olympics with a 5-2 win.

Latvian captain Karlis Skrastins (left) keeps his eye on the puck as Andrey Samokhvalov tries to keep him from getting to the airborne disc.

Switzerland 3 / Italy 3

February 21 • Palasport • 12:30 p.m.

Italy earned its first point of the tournament, on the last day of the round robin, as it held the surprising Swiss to a 3-3 tie. At the end of the game, the hometown fans gave their players a hearty standing ovation, just as they had for the women a few days earlier.

"We could have come out with better energy," said Switzerland's Paul DiPietro. "Aebischer kept us in it. When we play against a better team tomorrow, hopefully we rise to the challenge."

Indeed, goalie David Aebischer made 32 saves for La Suisse and at the other end Jason Muzzatti recorded 22 saves for Italy.

The Italians started out with fire in their eyes, hoping to finish the tournament on a winning note even though they were playing a team that had beaten Canada and Czech Republic. Despite their energetic burst out of the gate, the Swiss scored first, at 3:09, when Romano Lemm's shot beat Muzzatti to the glove side.

The Swiss went up 2-0 at 6:33 on a controversial goal scored by Patrick Fischer. A Martin Pluss shot deflected off Fischer and in, and after a video review referee Dennis LaRue ruled that Fischer had not deliberately kicked it in.

Italy narrowed the gap at 15:41 when Joe Busillo roofed a rebound off a Bob Nardella point shot on the power play. They tied the game just 53 seconds into the middle period, again on the power play. Carter

Trevisani's terrific slapshot beat Aebischer to the glove side while the goalie was screened.

Tony Iob gave Italy the lead at 6:13 of the third period when he popped a rebound over a lunging Aebischer who had made the original save on a shot by Giorgio de Bettin.

A win eluded the Italians, however, thanks to a bad giveaway in their own end by Busillo. His errant pass landed on the stick of Ivo Ruthemann directly in front of Muzzatti, and Ruthemann scored through the legs before the goalie could react. The goal came at 16:38 of the third.

"This was a learning stage we had to go through against the best teams," said Italy's coach, Mickey Goulet. "We hope to promote hockey in Italy. We may not have the skill of the NHL guys, but we have the same heart."

Patrick Fischer redirects Martin Pluss's shot past goalie Jason Muzzatti in the first period.

Niko Kapanen's shot eludes Robert Muller as four teammates watch.

Finland 2 / Germany 0

February 21 • Esposizioni • 3:30 p.m.

Although every game at the Olympics is important, some are more important than others. This wasn't one of them because Finland had already clinched first place in Group A and Germany had already been eliminated. For Finland, the main objective was to play well so as to keep the string of good performances going and to get out of the game without suffering any injuries. For Germany, the game was about learning and pride. Finland succeeded, winning the game 2-0, the team's fourth shutout in five games.

The Finns got on the scoresheet just 2:35 into the game. Already on a power play, they pulled goalie Fredrik Norrena on a delayed penalty, and on a rush into the German end Niklas Hagman made a great pass as he circled the net to Niko Kapanen in front. He one-timed a low shot between the pads of Robert Muller to make it 1-0.

The second period was fraught with whistles, plagued by tight checking, and bogged down by half-hearted performances. Christian Ehrhoff and Marcel Goc had mildly potent opportunities to score but were thwarted by Norrena, while the Finns played dump-and-chase and conservative offense to preserve the lead.

Even when referee Danny Kurmann tried to enliven matters by giving the Finns a troika of power plays there was little in the way of great shooting or big-time saves excepting one fine play by Ehrhoff who swept the puck away from his goal line after Muller lost sight of the puck. However, in the final minute Kurmann gave the Finns a five-on-three and on this they connected when Saku Koivu batted in a puck out of midair from the side of the goal.

In the third, the Finns took care of business, and that meant getting Norrena the shutout. Through five round-robin games, the team had scored 19 goals and allowed just two.

Slovakia 3 / Sweden 0

February 21 • Esposizioni • 8:00 p.m.

Slovakia defeated a listless Sweden team tonight 2-0 to finish atop Group B at the end of the preliminary round.

Goalie Mikael Tellqvist was making his Olympic debut in Turin. Coach Bengt Ake Gustafsson decided to rest his starter, Henrik Lundqvist, before tomorrow's quarter-finals. To make the fight fair Slovak coach Frantisek Hossa also started his backup, Karol Krizan.

The Swedes came out flat and didn't play particularly well or have many quality shots at Krizan. In fact, the top line of Peter Forsberg-Mats Sundin-Freddy Modin was well below par given the talent among that threesome.

However, the Slovaks came out clearly looking for the first goal. Marian Gaborik was stopped point blank by Tellqvist early in the period on a partial breakaway when the speedster tried to deke. But at 15:51 the Slovaks got the game's first goal when Peter Bondra drilled a rocket point shot on a power play that had just expired. The puck flew by Tellqvist's glove hand. This was a goal anytime, anywhere.

The Swedes had a two-man advantage for more than a minute and a half and Nicklas Lidstrom ripped a slapshot that hit the post and stayed in the crease. Krizan fell back to cover the puck. Apart from that, point shots were errant and passing too slow to capitalize on this great chance to tie the score.

Play opened after the Slovaks returned to full strength and Marian Hossa and Pavol Demitra had a two-on-the-goalie opportunity. They over-passed, though, and Tellqvist intercepted the puck. He then made two more fine pad saves to keep it a 1-0 game.

Early in the third, Tellqvist robbed Gaborik after the puck hit the post and stayed in the crease as happened in the first to Krizan. This time, the goalie reached back and put a glove on the puck before Gaborik could get to it.

Soon after failing to connect on a five-on-three, the Slovaks doubled their lead thanks to a great wrist shot while he was surrounded—but not checked--by three defending Swedes. A wrist shot by Radoslav Suchy from the slot with no one around upped the count to 3-0.

Sweden's goalie Mikael Tellqvist deftly breaks up a two-on-the-goalie pass from Pavol Demitra to Marian Hossa.

Alexander Korolyuk pulls away from the American defence and scores the game's first goal on a breakaway.

Russia 5 / USA 4

February 11 • Palasport • 8:30 p.m.

It began as a game Russia controlled and ended in a mad, third-period puck scramble that Russia almost lost. In the end of this entertaining contest the Russians prevailed 5-4 but not before the team blew leads of 3-1 and 4-3.

"Against the Russians it always seems like we have shootouts, and there's a lot of talent out there," said the USA's Doug Weight. The Americans used goalie Robert Esche tonight, and his performance was middling at best. Russia started Evgeni Nabokov and then coach Vladimir Krikunov inserted Maxim Sokolov for the final 40 minutes.

The goals parade began midway through the first when Alexander Korolyuk took the puck from Chris Drury at the Russian blueline and raced away on Esche. Korolyuk made a nice deke to the forehand and lifted it over the sliding goalie for a pretty goal.

The Russians struck again just a minute later on another pretty play. Evgeni Malkin and Darius Kasparaitis went in on a two-on-one, and a pass-pass-pass setup finished with the sensational Malkin tapping in the puck from the crease after a great play by Kasparaitis to get the puck over the stick of defenceman Brian Rafalski.

Down but not out, the Americans struck on a power play at 18:38 when Brian Rolston made good on a pass

from Craig Conroy back of the net. The second period was mostly Russia's, and it increased the lead to 3-1 on another great passing play, this by Pavel Datsyuk to Andrei Markov who nailed a shot over Esche's glove. Despite being badly outplayed, USA drew to within one again on a late power play goal from Brian Gionta, and this set the stage for a wild third period.

The fireworks began at 5:00 of the final period when Scott Gomez tied the game. A few minutes later, Alexander Ovechkin put Russia up once again on a beautiful pass from Malkin, and less than a minute later Erik Cole tied the game again for USA. The winner came from Alexei Kovalev just 74 seconds later, and the Russians hung on for the win.

Canada–Russia: A Retrospective

Jay Bouwmeester

In the 21st century, the Canada-Russia rivalry has had its finest moments at the World Junior Championships. In fact, Canada has played for the gold medal in all of the last five years (2002-2006), and in four of those (excepting 2004) their opponent was Russia. The Russians won in 2002 and 2003 by scores of 5-4 and 3-2, but in 2005 and 2006 the Canadians overpowered their rivals by 6-1 and 5-0 scores. What is important to note about those games is that several of the players from the early junior tournaments are with their respective teams in Turin.

Canada had Rick Nash and Jay Bouwmeester in 2002 while the Russians had Fedor Tyutin and Alexander Frolov. In 2003, Tyutin was back and Alexander Ovechkin played for the first time. Now playing at the highest level, they are set to face off against each other on the grandest stage of all, the Olympics.

At the senior level, Canada has enjoyed much recent success against the Russians. The last time they met was May 14, 2005, at the World Championship, an exciting game won 4-3 by Canada. In that game, the team jumped out to a 4-0 win only to fight tooth and nail to survive a furious Russian rally. In 2003, they also played at the World Championship, Canada dominating 5-2.

The teams never met at the 2004 World Cup, and back in 1996 they met only in the round robin of that year's World Cup, Canada winning

5-3. From an historical perspective, the Soviets have dominated Canada at the Olympics, but the last time the teams played each other was back in 1992 when the Unified Team replaced the Soviet Union in name and political designation for that tournament. That year Canada lost two games to their adversaries, 5-4 and 3-1. Prior to that, the nations played seven times, Canada losing all but one. Those results don't merit much consideration because Canada's amateurs played the best from CCCP in those years.

Alexander Frolov

There is nothing better in hockey than a Canada-Russia game. Since 1954 when the Soviet Union entered international play and shocked Canada at that year's World Championship, this rivalry has produced the most exciting and important games in hockey history, most notably, of course, the 1972 Summit Series.

In recent times, the top teams have rarely met. Canada avoided the Russians at Salt Lake in 2002 when USA won the semi-final showdown with Russia, and in 1998 the Czechs beat Canada in the semi-finals and met the Russians for gold.

Russia 2 / Canada 0

February 22 • Esposizioni • 8:30 p.m.

It was supposed to be good karma that Canada was playing its quarter-finals game against Russia in a building known affectionately as Espo. It was, after all, the play of Phil Esposito ("Espo") that carried Canada to victory over the Soviet Union in the historic Summit Series, but, alas, it was not to be.

Russia beat Canada 2-0 to advance to the semi-finals. Canada, gold medallists in 2002, was sent packing. If there were to be a better game in Turin, the two teams were going to have to play a game for the ages because this was a classic. "Every game helps get us to the finals," said Darius Kasparaitis. "We want a gold medal." For Canada, it was the third time in four games it was shutout.

It was Martin Brodeur in the Canadian net and Evgeni Nabokov in the Russian crease, and given the puck-shooting artisans in between it's not surprising they

Joe Sakic (left) and Alexei Yashin clash.

GAME SUMMARY

First Period
No Scoring

penalties: Afinogenov (Rus) 3:27, Zhukov (Rus) 5:36, Gagne (Can) 5:39, Pronger (Can) 8:35, Nash (Can) 11:44, Taratukhin (Rus) 15:38, Can (bench minor) 20:00

Second Period
No Scoring

penalties: Sushinsky (Rus) 3:05, Smyth (Can) 7:56, Richards (Can) 13:14, Ovechkin (Rus) 18:05

Third Period

#			
1	Russia, Ovechkin (*Kozlov*)		1:30
2	Russia, Kovalev (*Markov*)		19:37

penalties: Bertuzzi (Can) 0:55, Gonchar (Rus) 2:12, Kovalev (Rus) 5:13, Markov (Rus) 16:52, Lecavalier (Can) & Malkin (Rus—major, game misconduct) 18:59, Pronger (Can) 19:27

In Goal

Canada	Brodeur
Russia	Nabokov

Shots on Goal

Canada	7	9	11	**27**
Russia	11	16	6	**33**

Referee	Dennis LaRue (USA)
Linesmen	Joacim Karlsson (SWE)
	Tony Sericolo (USA)
Attendance	4,130

Despite playing an incredible game, goalie Martin Brodeur could not stop this shot by Alexander Ovechkin which gave Russia a 1-0 lead.

were kept busy all night long. Add to that Brodeur's added talent of puck handling as a third defenceman and he was perhaps the busiest man on the ice. Nontheless, it was Nabokov who made 27 stops for the shutout.

Joe Sakic ripped a quick wrist shot just wide on the opening shift, and Alexander Ovechkin made two dazzling rushes a bit later, one to draw a penalty, the other forcing Brodeur to make a fine glove save.

The tempo was frenzied and the fans contributed their support for their team, a crowd equally divided between the two hockey superpowers. The best save of the early going went to Brodeur who

whipped out his glove hand to stop a slap shot from the point moments after Shane Doan had done yeoman's work killing a few seconds off a Russian power play in the Russian end.

Canada lost Simon Gagne late in the period on a power play when he was hip-checked by Darius Kasparaitis, hip on knee, a power play that was created by the great work of the re-united power line of Joe Thornton-Rick Nash-Todd Bertuzzi. Gagne returned in the second.

Teams exchanged power-play chances to open the second, and while the Russians' advantage was ineffective, Canada had two fine chances on shots by Vincent Lecavalier and Bryan McCabe.

Playing five-on-five, action became more cautious and conservative. After a scoreless period, the opening goal became all the

more important. Russia had more puck possession, but Canada arguably had the better scoring chances. Every moment seemed like Russia was going to score because of puck movement, and every other moment favoured Canada for counter-attacking so dangerously. Canada finished off the period on a power play full of chances but couldn't convert, and after 40 minutes the game was still looking for its first goal.

The Russians struck early in the third after Todd Bertuzzi, a controversial selection to the team, took a penalty on Sergei Gonchar. The Canadians had possession behind their goal but couldn't clear and Viktor Kozlov fed Alexander Ovechkin in the slot. He drilled a high shot over the sprawling Brodeur to make it 1-0 Russia.

"In previous years it might not have been a penalty," Gonchar said, "but the way they call the game this year I knew right away it would be called."

It's almost impossible to describe the pace that ensued as a result of that goal. Canada pressed for the tying goal, and the Russians stormed back every chance they got. Canada maintained sustained pressure for long periods but could not beat Nabokov. The Russians ended the game with a last-minute power-play goal. They are off to the semi-finals.

"We wanted to be there at the end," Canadian captain Joe Sakic said. "We didn't generate enough scoring chances and we didn't capitalize. As the tournament went on, we got more tentative. We didn't work as a unit." ❧

Canada did everything but score against Russia, and that meant an early exit from the Olympics.

Sweden 6 / Switzerland 2

February 12 • Esposizioni • 4:30 p.m.

Sweden's predictable 6-2 win over Switzerland put the team in the semi-finals.

Tre Kronor struck first when P-J Axelsson's shot in the slot deflected off defenceman Steve Hirschi and between goalie Martin Gerber's pads for the opening goal.

A Sweden goal was to be expected, but what was less expected was that at 8:37 the Swiss tied the game, 1-1. Patric Della Rossa went behind the net to retrieve a loose puck and found Mark Streit in the slot. The Swiss captain ripped a great shot to Henrik Lundqvist's short side.

The Swiss were beset by more bad luck on a Sweden power play.

Peter Forsberg, at the right point, flicked a shot to the back side looking for Freddy Modin. Defenceman Olivier Keller swatted the pass away, but the puck hit Modin in the leg and dropped to his feet. He had only to lift the puck into the empty side as Gerber had moved over to play the original pass.

Two minutes later, the Swedes increased their lead to 3-1 when Henrik Zetterberg scored on a wraparound after drawing Gerber out of position.

The goal put the Swiss clearly on their heels and the Swedes took control. They went up 4-1 at 9:07 on the power play when Mats Sundin at the left point, took a pass from the other point and absolutely hammered a slapshot over the near shoulder of Gerber.

If there was any doubt about the outcome, Sundin erased that with another goal four minutes later when Forsberg made a beautiful seeing-eye pass to him in front and the captain redirected it past a shaky Gerber who was not having a 49-shot-shutout game as he had against Canada a few nights earlier.

Romano Leem for Switzerland and Daniel Alfredsson of Sweden rounded out the scoring in the third.

"We have only one goal," Alfredsson said, "and that's gold. We don't care who we meet in the semi-finals."

"We spent a lot of energy against Canada and the Czechs," Martin Pluss acknowledged, "and we just didn't have a lot today. After it was 3-1, it was very tough."

Action gets frenetic around Sweden's goal but Henrik Lundqvist keeps the puck out of this play.

Finland 4 / USA 3

February 12 • Palasport • 5:30 p.m.

By defeating USA 4-3, Finland advanced to a semi-final date with Russia.

"We all play in the same league, we do the same things, we drink the same beers," said Finland's Teemu Selanne of his nation's confidence when facing teams like the USA. "There's not that much difference. The gap between the number one team and the number eight team is not very big."

Finland got on the board at 9:33 when a Ville Peltonen shot squeezed through goalie Rick DiPietro's pads and trickled over the goal line. It was a well deserved lead, and despite a timeout call by USA to quell the tide, the Finns upped their lead just a few minutes later, shorthanded at that. Sami Salo's long slapshot just inside the Americans blueline tipped off Mathieu Schneider's stick and past DiPietro. Ironically, Schneider brought the American back in the game in the same way when his slapshot hit teammate Mike Knuble in the shoulder and past Antero Niittymaki.

Early in the second period, on another power play, Schneider tied the game with a shot from the top of the circle that found the net untouched. The celebrations were short-lived, though. Olli Jokinen scored on a Finnish power play on a bad-angle shot that DiPietro should have stopped.

Jokinen scored another on the power play at 17:10 of the second to make it 4-2 in a period that was end-to-end, wide-open hockey.

The USA made the game interesting late in the game. Chris Drury made a nice play to get the puck on goal while falling and Brian Gionta tipped it in to make it 4-3 with five minutes remaining.

The Americans pulled out all the stops in the final minutes but couldn't tie the game. DiPietro was pulled with 1:26 left, but despite puck possession in the Finnish end they couldn't get the tying goal. As a result, the Finns moved on and USA went home.

Olli Jokinen (#12 white) pops the puck into the net on a Finland power play in the second period to give his team a 3-2 lead.

Czech Republic 3 / Slovakia 1

February 12 • Esposizioni • 9:30 p.m.

The Czechs earned the final spot in the semi-finals with their win over Slovakia by 3-1, the last goal going into an empty net.

"Of course, after our preliminary round performances, I'm very sorry we lost this game," said Slovak coach Frantisek Hossa referring to his team's perfect 5-0-0 record leading up to the game. "We made some individual mistakes. Since yesterday we played against Sweden, maybe we were a little tired."

Milan Hnilicka was the surprise starter in goal for the Czechs and Peter Budaj was in goal again for the Slovaks.

The going early on was all on the periphery of the scoring areas, most of the play happening between the bluelines or in the corners.

Martin Rucinsky started the Czechs to victory midway through the period when he intercepted a pass in his own end while killing a penalty and beat Budaj on the breakaway.

"They dominated the first period," admitted Slovak defenceman Zdeno Chara. "We had a slow start and they caught us flat-flooted. They were skating and passing the puck and we were watching."

The Czechs doubled their lead at 8:41 of the second when Milan Hejduk got his stick on a loose puck in the crease and banged it home before anyone could check him. Slovakia had several chances to tie the game on the power play, but a combination of poor finish and good penalty killing produced no goals for the team.

Their lone goal came early in the third when Marian Gaborik blazed down the left side and blasted a wrist shot past Hnilicka. Martin Straka finished the scoring into an empty net as the Slovaks pushed for the tying goal.

Slovakia's Lubos Bartecko (in white) squeezes Jaromir Jagr along the boards.

What Went Wrong?

When Wayne Gretzky first became involved with Hockey Canada leading up to Salt Lake 2002 he stated emphatically that speed and skill were the first merits he would look for when considering players for the Olympics. He declared that Canada had as much individual talent in these regards as any other country in the world, and he went out and proved himself right. His mandate caught on, and players going to the World Championships and World Juniors were selected on similar merit without much concern for size and physical presence. Yet for 2006, Gretzky somewhat abandoned that objective in favour of experience and loyalty to those who had been loyal to Canadian hockey.

So, instead of choosing players such as Sidney Crosby, Jason Spezza, and Eric Staal—young, skilled, fast skaters—he went with Kris Draper, Shane Doan, and Chris Pronger, for instance.

Furthermore, the 2006 team had several players who had some accountability attached to their inclusion. Doan, for instance, was captain in Phoenix, where Gretzky coaches. Had Doan played for the Minnesota Wild or Florida Panthers, it would have been highly unlikely he would have been selected.

Todd Bertuzzi is another example. Maligned and roundly criticized for his seemingly career-ending attack on Steve Moore, he was given a chance to prove himself by Gretzky, the implied message being, 'I'm helping revive your reputation and career; now you help us win.'

Kris Draper has been loyal to Canada when asked to play at the World Championships, but his

Joe Thornton was one of many stars who failed to perform in Torino.

reputation is rooted in his abilities as a penalty killer. Spezza, Staal, Crosby are much more talented, but Draper's loyalty was rewarded. He didn't record a single point in Torino.

Bryan McCabe's inclusion was connected to his coach in Toronto, Pat Quinn. McCabe had had a great season to date, but much of his success was the result of playing the power play and unleashing accurate one-timer shots off soft passes across the blueline from Tomas Kaberle. Yet McCabe's play was so weak in Turin that he didn't play all that much on the power

play. He took silly penalties of his own and was a defensive liability.

In short, those players who owed Gretzky a strong performance didn't deliver, and virtually all the undisputed superstars—Joe Thornton, Joe Sakic, Rick Nash—simply didn't perform, either.

There were no team functions, no team support for the women's team or other Canadians at the Olympics. The team didn't play as one on the ice in part because it didn't live like one off it, as it had four years earlier. The result was seventh place.

Sweden 7 / Czech Republic 3

February 24 • Palasport • 4:30 p.m.

Sweden waltzed with unexpected ease to the gold-medal game by hammering the Czech Republic 7-3. Seven scorers each tallied for Tre Kronor. Apart from one stretch in the second period, Sweden was in control from start to finish and showed superior poise, confidence, and scoring ability. The loss means the Czechs play for the bronze medal against Russia.

Sweden has not been to the Olympic finals since 1994 when it won gold on Peter Forsberg's famous Kent Nilsson one-handed deke eluded Canadian goalie Corey Hirsch and Tommy Salo stopped Paul Kariya on the final shootout shot for victory.

This victory over the Czechs was ignited by a goal just 34 seconds from the opening whistle thanks to the best line of the night. Mats Sundin won the faceoff, and soon after the Swedes took the puck up ice. Peter Forsberg made a perfect cross-ice pass to Freddy Modin, and he blasted a one-timer past Milan Hnilicka who couldn't get over in time to block the shot.

Vaclav Prospal's backhander from in tight brought the score to 5-3 and gave the Czechs some hope.

Jorgen Jonsson's beautiful tip gave the Swedes a 5-1 lead in the second period.

The early goal allowed the Swedes to play their style of game, but their plan broke down when Filip Kuba tied the game just after the three-minute mark. Martin Straka skated inside the Sweden blueline and dropped the puck to Kuba. His shot went between Henrik Lundqvist's pads and trickled slowly over the line before he could reach back and grab it.

The quick goals put the teams back on even footing and they played more cautiously for several minutes. The Swedes regained the lead thanks to a pretty goal set up by defenceman Nicklas Lidstrom. With the puck at the point, he faked a big slapshot and instead passed hard to P-J Axelsson in front of Hnilicka. Axelsson redirected the puck perfectly to the top corner at 13:37 to give his team a lead it never relinquished. Early in the second Tre Kronor built up a 3-1 lead courtesy of another fine play, this a two-on-one featuring the Sedin twins. Henrik brought the puck in over the Czech blueline and fed a lovely pass to brother, Daniel. Although Hnilicka stopped him on the deke, Henrik was right there to poke in the rebound.

They put the game out of reach three minutes later when Daniel Alfredsson made a pinpoint pass from behind the net to Christian Backman and his shot eluded Hnilicka.

Jorgen Jonsson replicated the P-J Axelsson goal when he tipped a Kenny Jonsson pass in similar fashion past the goalie, and by this point, Czech coach Alois Hadamczik made a change in net and put in Tomas Vokoun. Now down 5-1, the Czechs rallied briefly thanks to some penalty trouble by the Swedes. During a five-on-three, Jaromir Jagr blasted a shot wide, but the rebound came out the other side right onto the stick of Ales Hemsky who put it into the open side of the net.

Less than a minute later, Vaclav Prospal tipped a shot past Lundqvist on a rush to bring the score to 5-3. The momentum was all going their way, and it was abetted by a four-minute high-sticking minor to Niklas Kronwall for a foul on Martin Rucinsky. If the Czechs were going to rally, this was the time.

The Swedes, though, did a superb job killing the penalty and before the period ended they beat Vokoun for the first time to go up 6-3 heading to the dressing room. This time it was Axelsson making the behind-the-net pass and Alfredsson in front snapping home the goal. In the third, it was all Sweden. The team played perfect defense and added their seventh goal thanks to a Henrik Zetterberg pass to Tomas

Holmstrom to make the score all the more convincing.

Solid Swedish checking dampened Czech hopes of a comeback the rest of the way. Henrik Zetterberg's perfect pass to Tomas Holmstrom for a one-timer goal off the rush with 3:05 left provided Sweden with some insurance.

The Swedes wave to the fans after their convincing 7-3 win that took them to the gold-medal game.

Finland 4 / Russia 0

February 24 • Palasport • 8:30 p.m.

Finland scored goals in every period and Antero Niittymaki posted the shutout as Suomi dominated Russia en route to a gold-medal showdown with neighbour and nemesis Sweden. The 4-0 score was every bit indicative of the edge in play. The gold-medal game will be played Sunday afternoon at Palasport.

The teams started out playing tentative versions of their distinctive styles, the Finns extra cautious and perhaps overly respectful of Russia's speed, the Russians not trying anything fancy at the Finnish blueline for fear of a turnover.

The game's first big break came via a Finnish power play when Kimmo Timonen simply drifted a point shot toward the goal. The puck was deftly tipped in front by Teemu Selanne at 6:14, and the goal gave the Finns life after their conservative start. They drew another penalty just a few seconds later, and although they didn't increase the lead, Olli Jokinen had two great chances and gave the Finns momentum and confidence.

Teams tried challenging each other's strategies. The Russians got around the neutral-zone trap by dumping the puck in, something they are loathe to do. Once in, they were successful at gaining possession and creating opportunities. When they tried to carry the puck in against a disciplined Finnish defence, they were far less successful.

The Finns were equally successful at maintaining puck control once they managed to penetrate the Russian blueline. As a result, most of the period was spent inside the bluelines instead of between them.

"When we play as a team and within our system, we can beat anybody," Jarkko Ruutu suggested. "Russia's weakness is that they have a lot of individual skills, but they're not playing as a team. So, when you play against a good team like we've been all tournament, there's a difference. You create turnovers and capitalize on them. You don't really care who scores. All you care about is the win."

Russian Alexei Kovalev tries the wraparound but goalie Antero Niittymaki and Teemu Selanne prevent a goal.

Alexander Ovechkin had a great chance when he barreled down the right side and cut in on goalie Antero Niittymaki, but the goalie stood his ground and kicked aside the shot.

At the other end, Niklas Hagman rattled a puck off the post past a beaten Nabokov, but the puck stayed out. Moments later, Ville Peltonen had a chance close-in but was again stymied by the goalie.

The second period, like the first, began slowly. The Russians, for all their speed, were kept to the outside by the defending Finns and couldn't get any good chances on Niittymaki.

The Finns struck on a counter-attack at 9:33. Selanne stole the puck at centre ice and carried

Although Olli Jokinen didn't score on this play, he did get a goal in Finland's 4-0 win over Russia.

the puck in, taking the initial shot. Saku Koivu picked up the rebound, twisted away from his check and fired a perfect pass in the slot to Toni Lydman. Despite being covered, Lydman drilled a one-timer past a shocked Nabokov, and the Finns now led 2-0.

The Finns spent most of the rest of the period chipping the puck out of their end and chasing it, relieving pressure before it allowed for a Russians scoring chance. They managed another goal on a power play when Timonen's point shot bounced off the backboards directly into the crease where it bounced off defenceman Andrei Markov's leg and into the net. Saku Koivu was right there and was given credit for the goal, and the 3-0 lead after 40 minutes seemed almost insurmountable

given the Finns had allowed just five goals in six games and two periods.

In order to get through the period, though, the Finns killed off a five-on-three for almost two full minutes. Frustrated and unable to make passes from side to side, the Russians resorted to slapshots from the point for their scoring chances, and the three skaters and Niittymaki happily defended this offense. It was an impressive display by Suomi, to say the least.

The third was an even starker contrast than the second as the Finns, sensing victory, had no interest in the Russian goal. Their only aim was to keep the puck out of their own end, and the Russians, evermore frustrated, tried longer and longer passes, more desperate passes, and lower percentage passes.

They got their fourth goal on the counter attack again as Peltonen passed cross ice to Jokinen on the rush, a beautiful goal at 9:17 that sealed the victory.

It was Finland's fifth shutout in seven games, and the team has allowed just six goals so far en route to the finals.

Said captain Saku Koivu: "We certainly didn't expect to win like this. They're a talented team, but our defense was excellent. We could see in the second and third period they were getting frustrated. This is the dream final against our most hated rivals."

Lord Stanley Visits Torino

Phil Pritchard and Craig Campbell, curators from the Hockey Hall of Fame in Toronto, took the Stanley Cup to Torino as part of the Olympic celebration of hockey. For most of the week it was in the city, the cherished trophy stayed at the House of Hockey, the IIHF's headquarters during the Olympics. One afternoon, however, Pritchard and Campbell took the Cup downtown for visitors to see. Needless to say, it was a huge success.

Czech Republic 3 / Russia 0

February 25 • Palasport • 8:30 p.m.

It was a game neither team wanted to play, but the Czechs wanted the bronze medal more than the Russians and played with more intensity. The result was a 3-0 win to claim third place in men's hockey. Tomas Vokoun recorded the shutout for the Czechs.

"I was in net when we won the World Championship last year and I played in all of the games," Vokoun explained of the satisfying victory. "But I came here and the coach lost faith in me, I guess, and I didn't start in the semi-finals. In the end, I have a medal from the Olympics."

Captain Robert Lang earned his third Olympic medal (bronze in 1992 and gold in 1998) and contributed two assists to the win.

The Russians, meanwhile, which started the tournament flying down the ice scoring pretty goals, were shut out for the second straight game. "We had our chances but we couldn't put the puck in the net," defenceman Darius Kasparaitis said. "We had a better team, I think. We just couldn't score."

"We had good mental preparation before the game, but the first quick goal broke our players' confidence," said Russian coach Vladimir Krikunov. "They played their best but unfortunately without goals."

"Vokoun is a great goalie, but so is Martin Brodeur, and we scored twice on him," said Danny Markov. "It doesn't matter how many opportunities you have—20, 10, five. When you score, it's good."

The Czechs score the game's first goal at 4:48 when David Vyborny made a nice pass to Martin Erat. He drilled a one-timer while Nabokov was sliding over to cover the shot, but the puck flew over his shoulder and in.

A Russian scrum in front of Czech goalie Tomas Vokoun failed to produce a goal.

Alexander Kharitonov rings a shot off the post.

A short time later the Russians almost tied the game when Maxim Afinogenov busted up the middle and drilled a shot off the post that had Vokoun cleanly beaten. The team also failed to capitalize on three power plays in the first.

Ilya Kovalchuk caused a fury early in the second period when he smashed defenceman Pavel Kubina into the boards. The hit left Kubina dazed and bloodied. He left the game and didn't return to action, but he did stand near the bench as time wound down to be part of the medal presentations.

"I feel tired and a little dizzy," Kubina said after, the bronze medal dangling from his neck. "We scored on the power play, so I guess something good came from it."

Indeed, Kovalchuk was given a five-minute major for boarding and a match penalty. He scored four goals in the Olympics, all in the one game against Latvia during a 9-2 rout.

The Czechs upped their lead on the extended power play. Marek Zidlicky took a point shot that goalie Evgeni Nabokov couldn't see, and the 2-0 lead seemed solid given the team's ability to keep the Russian speedsters on the perimeter of play.

"They play such good defence, it's tough to score," Nabokov said. "When we beat Canada, we played team hockey, but today we played individual hockey. They took our speed away, our passing lanes, away."

Despite a 12-2 margin of shots in the third period in favour of the Russians they couldn't beat Vokoun.

At least, not legally. With fewer than four minutes left in the game, they thought they scored when Pavel Datsyuk batted the puck out of mid-air and past Vokoun, but the video review indicated Datsyuk's stick was above the level of the crossbar and the game remained 2-0.

Martin Straka completed the scoring with an empty netter at 19:52.

The Czechs were presented their medals by Jari Kurri, arguably the greatest Finn of all time and a member of the IOC. The Finnish general manager of these Olympics was accompanied by IIHF Council Members Hans Dobida of Austria and Frederick Meredith of Great Britain.

Sweden Prepares for Glory

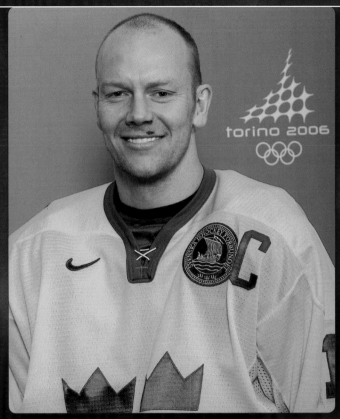

Captain Mats Sundin.

It's a rivalry made in heaven—or perhaps hell.

"Sweden-Finland is like Canada-U.S. or Czechs and Slovaks," Swedish defenceman Kenny Jonsson said after practice today, the team's final preparation before tomorrow afternoon's gold-medal showdown with Finland to close out the Olympics.

Jonsson is one of just three players from the 1994 gold-medal team, the first and only Olympic gold for Tre Kronor. "I have a lot of good memories from that year. Forsberg's goal. The save at the end by Salo. There were 100,000 people in Stockholm waiting for us when we arrived home. It was very special, and at the time you think it's once in a lifetime. It helps get us some positive energy for tomorrow's game." The two other survivors from 1994 are Peter Forsberg, whose spectacular goal won the gold in the shootout, and Jorgen Jonsson, a veteran now of 253 national games leading up to tomorrow.

"To be honest," captain Mats Sundin said, "we've all played them so many times in our careers, it's not like it will be something different. What's nice is to be playing in a gold-medal game at the Olympics. What we know about Finland is that it's always a tough game when we play them."

"I think if you bet ten dollars on a Finland-Sweden finals before the Olympics began," Daniel Alfredsson suggested, "you wouldn't have had much company.

are six or seven teams that could win gold, and we're happy to be where we are. Our whole focus now is on tomorrow."

"A good start is extremely important for us," he explained. "We have to be smart. We can't turn the puck over, and we have to stay patient. I think the Russians got a little frustrated the other day. We can't do that. They [the Finns] don't give up a lot of scoring chances. Also, we have to stay out of the penalty box because they have a great power play. So do we, though. I think whoever wins the specialty teams will have the best

To reduce the game to its bare essentials, though, Sweden has to master one difficulty: How do you score against a team that has recorded five shutouts in seven games and has surrendered just five goals in total?

"I'll be very happy if we win 1-0, so we only have to score once," coach Bengt Ake Gustafsson said without so much as a friendly grin. "We've been able to score goals here, so I'm not worried." What about shutting down a potent counter attack like the Finns? "We have pretty good defence tactics, too," Gustafsson continued in

Sweden 3 / Finland 2

February 26 • Palasport • 2:00 p.m.

Nicklas Lidstrom's spectacular slapshot goal ten seconds into the third period on fresh ice broke a 2-2 tie and gave Sweden gold-medal victory this afternoon at Palasport.

Sweden is the new Olympic champion. The country's only other gold came in 1994. Three players in Turin were on that team 12 years ago: Peter Forsberg, Jorgen Jonsson, and Kenny Jonsson.

It was clear from the opening faceoff that this was going to be a battle of systems, the Swedes and Finns both emphasizing defence first and scoring opportunities second. Thankfully, referee Paul Devorski helped kick start the action in the third minute of the game when he sent off Niklas Havelid for a routine hooking penalty. It was the Swedes, though, who had the two best scoring chances while playing short-handed.

The first came when Mikael Samuelsson did some fine work in the Finns' corner and wafted the puck out to the blueline where Nicklas Lidstrom walked into a slapshot that he drilled wide. The second was a nice shot by P-J Axelsson that goalie Antero Niittymaki hugged in his belly.

After a harmless Sweden power play the Finns struck with the game's first bit of excitement. Jorgen Jonsson took a penalty, and on the ensuing power play Kimmo Timonen's point shot skipped between Henrik Lundqvist's legs and over the red line at 14:45. Saku Koivu was doing some spadework in front and was initially credited with the goal.

Nicklas Lidstrom celebrates his go-ahead goal early in the third. It proved to be the gold-medal goal.

Ville Peltonen scored the 2-2 goal fro Finland in the second period.

Another penalty, this to Freddy Modin, put the Swedes on their heels even further though they survived the man shortage.

The Finns played defence to perfection. They never allowed an odd-man rush; they recovered most of Sweden's dump-ins, and they held play up at their blueline so that oncoming Swedes frequently had to straddle the blueline to avoid going offside while a teammate looked for a lane to get the puck deep. The Finns played as a five-man unit inside their line, as they had all tournament.

The Swedes broke through on their own power play at 4:42 of the second with Toni Lydman in the penalty box. Henrik Zetterberg took a pass behind Niittymaki's goal and swung quickly out front. His

shot bounced off the goalie's pad and in. The goal was as important psychologically for Sweden as it was on the scoreboard, the magical Finnish defence fallible after all and the great Niittymaki not as perfect as he had been all tournament.

Sweden had two more power plays in quick order, building on the momentum created by their tying goal. Niittymaki made a great toe save on a Freddy Modin blast, but Lundqvist also stopped Jere Lehtinen in similar fashion at the other end of the ice.

Slowly but surely, the Swedes started to use their speed and passing to generate some offense and get the puck to the goal. They finally got the go-ahead goal on the power play on a rare Finnish error in the slot. Zetterberg fired a pass

to Niklas Kronwall but the puck was a bit behind him. Antti Laaksonen was lazy in checking Kronwall and the Swede recovered the puck as he lost his balance. His quick shot beat Niittymaki low to the stick side, and for the first time since the first period of their game against the Czechs, the Finns trailed on the scoreboard.

The Tre Kronor lead didn't last long--a minute and a half, to be precise. Jussi Jokinen made a great pass out front to Ville Peltonen. He was lazily checked by Kronwall and Peltonen made no mistake in close at 15:00.

Peltonen had a great chance to restore the lead for Finland but he blasted a slot shot wide of Lundqvist. The period ended with Finland having gotten back into the game.

The third period started like lightning for Sweden. Nicklas Lidstrom trailed Mats Sundin coming in over the Finnish blueline, and Sundin dropped the puck for his defenceman. Lidstrom blew a point shot over the stick-side shoulder of Niittymaki just ten seconds in, the fresh ice surely helping the puck travel a bit faster. The odd-man rush was made possible when Saku Koivu broke his stick at the opening faceoff and had to race to the bench to get a new one.

They were not going to be so glib with their lead this time. Right after the goal, Tre Kronor settled in to a defensive style, content first and foremost with preventing any Finnish offensive chances. Of course, midway through the period, still trailing, the Finns had to open the game up, and this led to great end-to-end hockey.

Niklas Hagman had a great chance from the high slot but his hard shot caught the shoulder of Lundqvist and bounced into the corner. It was their best chance of the period.

Niittymaki left the Finnish goal with 90 seconds left for a sixth attacker, but to no avail. The Finns attacked Lundqvist with all their energy but the Swedish defence was just a bit better. Time expired before Suomi could count the tying goal.

The official team photo.

Every Swede is around the Tre Kronor net as Finland pushed for the tying goal late in the game.

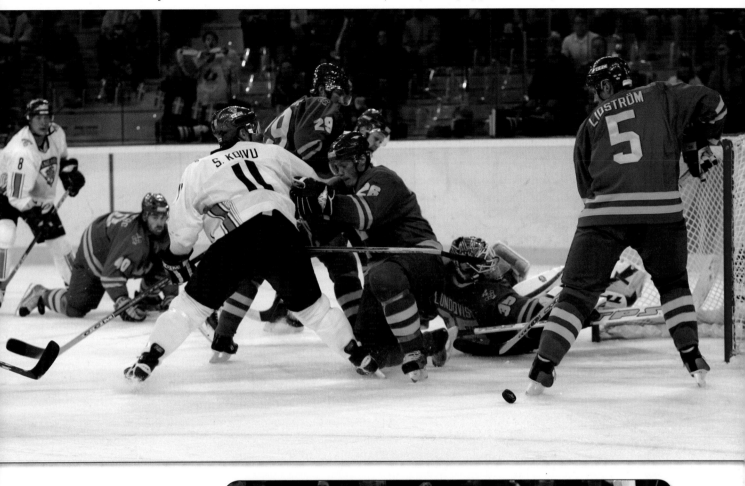

Gold medal hugs for Tre Kronor.

New World Rankings

By virtue of their gold medal, the Swedes assumed the number-one ranking that Canada had held for nearly three years.

For the first time since this system was introduced after the 2003 World Championship, the IIHF's World Rankings have a new name at the top of the standings. By advancing to the gold-medal game, Sweden has overtaken Canada as the number-one men's hockey nation. The World Rankings take into account countries' performance over a continuous four-year cycle. The current year (in this case, the Olympics) counts for 100% of total points available, the previous year 75%, two years ago 50%, and three years ago 25%. The maximum points available is 1,200 which is awarded to the champion. Here are the top ten nations on the men's side after the Olympics.

These will no doubt change in May following the 2006 World Championship in Riga, Latvia.

1	Sweden	4,030
2	Canada	3,940
3	Czech Republic	3,930
4	Slovakia	3,805
5	Finland	3,765
6	Russia	3,725
7	USA	3,575
8	Switzerland	3,525
9	Latvia	3,335
10	Germany	3,270

For the women, Canada and USA were tied prior to the Olympics, but USA received superior placement because it defeated Canada at last year's World Championship. With the gold medal in Torino, however, Canada regains first place. The top eight women's nations after the Olympics looks as follows. These are final for 2006:

1	Canada	2,970
2	USA	2,890
3	Sweden	2,830
4	Finland	2,760
5	Germany	2,635
6	Russia	2,585
7	China	2,485
8	Switzerland	2,480

1920

Antwerp, Belgium
April 23-September 12, 1920 —(Winter Olympics held April 23–29, 1920)

GOLD	CANADA
Silver	United States
Bronze	Czechoslovakia
Fourth	Sweden

TEAM CANADA: Winnipeg Falcons

Wally Byron, Bobby Benson, Konnie Johannesson, Frank Fredrickson (*captain*), Chris Fridfinnson, Mike Goodman, Slim Halderson, Allan "Huck" Woodman, Gordon Sigurjonsson (*coach*), Hebbie Axford (*manager*), William Hewitt (*secretary*)

The Winnipeg Falcons

The Canadian Olympic Committee felt that the group of amateur players most deserving to represent Canada—and the team most likely to win—would be Canada's amateur titleists, the Allan Cup champions. To qualify for the Allan Cup finals, the Falcons whipped the Fort William Maple Leafs in Winnipeg by scores of 7–2 and 9–1 before carrying on to Toronto to play Varsity (the University of Toronto team) in a two-game total-goals series for amateur supremacy in Canada and the right to travel to Belgium as Canada's national hockey team. The result was that the Varsity team was hammered 8–3 on March 28 and 3–2 the following night before a stunned Hogtown crowd. The Falcons were Allan Cup champions and on their way to Belgium.

The Trip

Just getting to the host city was a significant part of Olympic participation in the early days of the Games. The total cost of the Falcons' voyage from Canada to Antwerp was estimated at $10,000, a colossal sum that was collected from Allan Cup receipts as well as from handsome donations from both the Manitoba government ($2,000) and the City of Winnipeg ($500). After winning the Allan Cup, the Falcons carried on directly from Toronto to Ottawa and then to Montreal, where they were welcomed by William Northey, Allan Cup trustee, and members of the Montreal AAA (Amateur Athletic Association) team. The Falcons arrived in Saint John, New Brunswick on April 3, where they boarded the CPR steamship SS *Melita* two days later.

The Winnipeg Falcons, Canada's representatives at the first Olympic hockey tournament, 1920.

Hockey at the Olympics

There were two equally influential reasons why hockey was finally made an Olympic event for the first time at these 1920 Summer Games. (The first Olympic Winter Games were held in 1924.) One reason was that for the first time the International Olympic Committee was able to secure commitments to compete from at least five European nations — Belgium, France, Switzerland, Sweden, and the newly created Czechoslovakia (Germany and Austria, because of their involvement in World War I, were not allowed to participate in these Games). The second reason was that the managers of Antwerp's Le Palais de Glace stadium refused to allow their building to be used for figure skating unless hockey were included in the package! Because these two conditions took time to arrange, it was not until mid-January that the competing nations (the five European ones, as well as Canada and the United States) were informed of the event's inclusion in the Olympics.

The only known sweater from Canada's 1920 Olympic hockey team.

The Finish and Return

On the evening of April 27, after winning the gold medal the previous day, the Falcons were feted royally as guests of the Canadian Pacific ocean service officers in Antwerp. Two nights later, the team received their medals, and after the ceremony Mike Goodman gave a performance of trick-skating during a hugely popular show by the figure skaters. The appreciative crowd demanded an encore from Goodman, and only Goodman.

After departing Antwerp, the players visited the battlefields of Belgium and France before carrying on to Paris, where Winnipeg Mayor Waugh was awaiting their arrival with a sumptuous banquet prepared in their honour. Frank Fredrickson and team coach Gordon Sigurjonsson left for Iceland, while the rest of the team set sail from Le Havre on May 5 aboard the SS *Grampian*. Their departure was something of a miracle as all seamen and dock workers were on strike. Le Havre was a madhouse, and the *Grampian* was the only vessel to leave as scheduled.

Gold medal from 1920 Olympics.

Ten days later the Falcons reached Quebec City. They went directly to Montreal and the next day to Toronto, where they were honoured non-stop for the balance of the day, beginning with lunch given by the Sportsmen's Patriotic Association.

Later, they were guests of the City of Toronto at the Royal York Hotel, where Mayor Tommy Church welcomed the team with open arms, gifts, stories, and entertainment. Sheriff Paxton presented William Hewitt with a monocle to complete the team secretary's formal attire. After Jack Slack sang a few songs, Mayor Church invited everyone to a night of boxing. He reminded them that the first fight on the card was scheduled for 8:30pm sharp, and they all proceeded to the Arena Gardens (Mutual Street Arena).

The final celebration, of course, awaited the team in their home town. The Falcons reached Winnipeg on May 22 and were given a huge parade downtown leading to Wesley College field where they were presented the Allan Cup. After the ceremonies, the team was given its final banquet of the season, at the Fort Garry Hotel before some 400 honoured guests. The World's Champions then settled down to enjoy a peaceful summer.

Cup given to William Hewitt after returning home.

100

1924

Chamonix, France
January 25-February 5, 1924

GOLD	CANADA
Silver	United States
Bronze	Great Britain
Fourth	Sweden
Fifth (Tie)	Czechoslovakia
	France
Seventh (Tie)	Belgium
	Switzerland

TEAM CANADA: **Toronto Granites**

Jack Cameron, Ernie Collett, Dunc Munro (*captain*), Beattie Ramsay, Hooley Smith, Cyril "Sig" Slater, Harry Watson, Bert McCaffery, Harold McMunn, Frank Rankin (*coach*), William Hewitt (*general manager*)

The Toronto Granites

The Granites was a team formed by ex-servicemen from the Great War. From the time they began competing in the Ontario Hockey Association (OHA) in 1919–20 until they disbanded (after the 1924 Olympics), the team was virtually unbeatable. They won the John Ross Robertson Cup in 1920, 1922, and 1923 (OHA Senior champions) and were runners-up to the University of Toronto in 1921.

The team qualified as Canada's 1924 Olympic representatives by winning the Allan Cup in successive seasons. In 1922, they beat the Regina Victorias 6–2 and 7–0 in games played in Toronto, and in 1923 they beat the University of Saskatchewan 11–2. However, some Granite players from these teams—Alex Romeril, Hugh Fox, Don Jeffrey, and Jack Aggett—were unable to make the trip overseas and were replaced by amateurs from the west (Harold McMunn from Winnipeg's Falcon Hockey Club) and east (Sig Slater from Montreal's Victoria Hockey Club).

Once the final roster had been established, the team played exhibition games against the best amateur teams in Toronto, Hamilton, Sault Ste. Marie, London, Niagara Falls, Ottawa, Kingston, and Montreal, finishing their tour with a sound 4–1 win over the Abeyweits of Charlottetown in a game played at Saint John, New Brunswick.

The Olympics

All games were played outside, on natural ice, on a European size rink, quite unfamiliar to the Canadians who were used to smaller confines that created a more physical game.

Beattie Ramsay goes in on goal.

The Toronto Granites, Canada's representatives in 1924.

Also, the boards were only about a foot high, thus preventing the Canadians from using them with the skill they did back home, particularly for hitting and passing. Additionally, netting was put up at both ends to prevent the "loss" of pucks. Ice conditions were often so poor that the boards had to be relocated almost daily to ensure the best possible patch of ice was being used!

From the time the Granites arrived, the weather varied in the extreme, from warm sun to heavy rain. These conditions were not ideal for hockey, and the Canadians were unable to have even one practice to acclimatise themselves to the already alien rink. On January 25, they made an attempt to skate but were quickly whisked off the ice after complaints from Norway, Sweden, and Finland, all of which claimed Canada had not scheduled the practice. In order to stay in shape, the Canadians did road work, running and the like. None of these obstacles hampered the team, which was vastly superior to the competition and easily retained the gold medal the Winnipeg Falcons had won for Canada at the 1920 Olympics at Antwerp.

Superfluous Tending of Goal

Such was the strength of the Canadian team that goaler Jack Cameron had a tough time maintaining his interest in games that saw him literally idle from start to finish. Legend has it that Cameron frequently skated to the boards to chat up the young ladies who were in attendance. Later in life, he denied the allegations but did impart one interesting anecdote: "The only girl I remember," he recalled, "was a little blonde 11-year old figure skater on the Norwegian team. When she wasn't competing, she sat on our bench. Her name was Sonja Henie and she was a great booster of the Granites." The pulchritudinous Henie finished last in competition that year, but in the next Games she dazzled the world with her gold-medal-winning performance and went on to become both a professional skater and popular film star.

The Finals

Even before play to decide the gold medal between the Canadians and Americans began, there was controversy. Both William Hewitt and W. S. Haddock, managers for the Canadians and Americans, respectively, refused the official proposal to draw the referee's name from a hat. Both men agreed that choosing an official from among the continental countries competing (Britain, France, Sweden, Belgium, Switzerland, and Czechoslovakia) would likely leave this important game in the hands of an inexperienced man. In the end, negotiations resulted in Hewitt proposing Paul Loicq of Belgium and Haddock selecting La Croix of France. Hewitt objected that La Croix might be related to the American goalie of the same name. A coin toss settled the argument, and Loicq became the referee.

There was clearly an air of animosity to the game, created in part by Harry Watson's remark earlier that Canada would win 10 or 12 to nothing. Less than two minutes after the puck had been faced off, Watson was bleeding from the nose and American Willard Rice had been knocked out by Smylie's stick. By the end of the game, the Americans were exhausted and gasping for breath and the Canadians tired but victorious thanks to the heroic and skilful play of their star forward trio of Watson, Smith, and McCaffery.

1928 ST. MORITZ, SWITZERLAND

February 11-20, 1928

GOLD	CANADA
Silver	Sweden
Bronze	Switzerland
Fourth	Great Britain
Fifth	France
Sixth	Czechoslovakia
Seventh (Tie)	Belgium
	Austria

TEAM CANADA: **University of Toronto Graduates**

Norbert "Stuffy" Mueller, Dr. Joe Sullivan, Frank Fisher, Rogers "Rod" Plaxton, John "Red" Porter (*captain*), Ross Taylor, Dr. Lou Hudson, Dave Trottier, Hugh Plaxton, Charlie Delahey, Bert Plaxton, Grant Gordon, Frank Sullivan, Conn Smythe (*coach*), William Hewitt (*manager*)

U of T Grads pose for a team photo in St. Moritz, Switzerland.

The University of Toronto Graduates

The formation of the team was as simple as its name implies—a group of players who graduated from the U of T and went on to establish themselves in the Ontario Hockey Association. After winning the OHA title, the Grads travelled to Vancouver to meet Fort William in the Allan Cup finals. They won, but the scores were close, the first a 2–2 tie, then a 3–2 overtime loss and 4–1 win to force an unusual, tie-breaking, fourth game, which the Grads won 2–1 (after 20 minutes of overtime) and with it the right to represent Canada at the Olympics.

To prepare themselves for international competition, the Grads spent most of January playing exhibition matches to hone their skills. They played the University Club of Boston in Boston before returning to Canada to play teams en route to Halifax, where they would set sail for St. Moritz. They played in Dunnville, Ontario, on January 11, London on the 14th, Toronto the 16th, Kingston the 18th, the Vics in Montreal the 19th, and Halifax the 21st. They lost only once all month, the

second game against Boston, and this marked but the third time in two years the team had been beaten (by the Marlies in S.P.A. competition 4–3 the previous year, and the aforementioned 3–2 loss to Fort William in the Allan Cup series in Vancouver on March 28, 1927).

The last game in Canada was particularly satisfying for the team. They encountered heavy snowstorms and drifts from Montreal to Halifax via Moncton, but although tired and despite going straight from the station to the rink, the team was roused by an enormous crowd of 8,000 packed into the new Forum. The Grads played an all-star team from the Maritimes and won handily, and the fans were further treated to a speed-skating race featuring Dave Trottier and Ross Taylor of the Grads against two Maritimers. Trottier won the race in 16 seconds (in a building the size of Maple Leaf Gardens). His first prize was a silver cigarette case. In addition, all Olympians received a pen knife by way of "good luck" from their Halifax supporters. The next day, January 22, they set sail at 4:00pm aboard the Red Star liner SS *Arabic*.

The hockey rink was contained within the dimensions of the speed skating oval.

Game action during Canada's gold medal performance.

Team Canada practices in St. Moritz.

The Team, Altered

Controversy crept into the Grads' preparations when coach Conn Smythe was not allowed to add two players—Wes Kirkpatrick and Dick Richards—to the Olympic roster for St. Moritz. Two of his players—Joe Sullivan and Hugh Plaxton—lobbied over Smythe's head to get their relatives on the squad instead, threatening to boycott the Games if their brothers were not selected to the Olympic team. Smythe was livid and refused to go overseas without the men to whom he had promised positions. However, Frank Sullivan, Bert Plaxton, and Rogers Plaxton were put on the team and Kirkpatrick, Richards, and Smythe remained in Canada.

The Post-Olympic Exhibition

After the gold medal triumph, the Grads took their remarkable show on the European road, as it were. They played in Vienna, Berlin, Paris, and London, the last leg of their whirlwind tour, before heading home. While in London, they were given a dinner and dance following their game and left for Liverpool on March 9. The next day, they boarded the *Celtic*, the world's largest liner, back to Canada. While on board, all passengers were asked to look out for a plane flown by W.R. Hinchcliffe and Elsie Mackay, a brave couple who were trying to follow in the transatlantic footsteps of Charles Lindbergh. Sadly, the plane was never spotted and the couple never found.

Exactly a week later, the Grads docked at Halifax and were promptly whisked off to an arena for another exhibition game. They travelled to Toronto via Quebec City and Montreal and were met at Union Station by a huge procession of University of Toronto students who marched them up Bay Street through a ticker-tape parade to City Hall. On March 22, the last in an exhausting line of honours, the Grads were given a dinner by the University of Toronto Sports Club attended by Conn Smythe, U of T president Robert Falconer, P.J. Mulqueen (Canadian Olympic Committee chairman), and all the athletes from the U of T.

Postscript

Dr. Lou Hudson, the team's right winger, later became friends with the Barilko family in Timmins. It was Lou's brother, Henry, who piloted the Fairchild 24 plane that went missing August 27, 1951, while he and Leaf hero Bill Barilko were flying to the far north on a fishing expedition. Lou had originally planned to join the two, but the weight of the three men might have been too much for the small plane and he stayed home. The wreck was not discovered until January 6, 1962.

1932 Lake Placid, New York

February 4–13, 1932

GOLD	CANADA
Silver	United States
Bronze	Germany
Fourth	Poland

TEAM CANADA: The Winnipegs

William Cockburn (*captain*), Stanley Wagner, Roy Hinkel, Hugh Sutherland, George Garbutt, Walter Monson, Harold "Hack" Simpson, Bert "Spunk" Duncanson, Romeo Rivers, Aliston "Stoney" Wise, Clifford Crowley, Victor Lindquist, Norm Malloy, Kenneth Moore, Jack Hughes (*coach*), Lou Marsh (*manager*)

The Winnipeg Hockey Club

In the first three Olympics, Canada had no trouble winning the gold medal each time. The teams representing the country were dominant and performed with the brilliance that was expected of them. However, the nomination of the Winnipeg Hockey Club to represent Canada in Lake Placid did not arouse the usual optimism. Far from it. Right from the get-go this was seen as a weak team, one that had won the Allan Cup convincingly over the Hamilton Tigers a year ago and that was current senior Canadian champion, to be sure, but somehow lacking the lustre and superiority of previous winners.

More specifically, the Canadian Olympic Association was worried about the lack of scoring ability on the team and was strongly in favour of adding players to the Winnipegs at the last minute to remedy this deficiency. To wit, they lost two games 1–0 and tied another 0–0 in the weeks leading up to the Games during competition in the Winnipeg City League in which they played (a total of six goals in seven league games), and the COA felt it had precedent on its side in wanting to alter the roster of a team going to the Olympics. When Hugh Fox, Alex Romeril, Jack Aggett, and Don Jeffrey could not accompany their Toronto Granites mates for the 1924 Games, Harold McMunn and Sig Slater were added to the club at the last minute. On the positive side, the Winnipegs had allowed only three goals in those seven league games and were considered the finest defensive team ever to play in Canada.

In this spirit, Walter Monson and Norm Malloy of the Senior A Selkirk Fisherman, and Bert Duncanson, a noted Junior A star, were added to this 1932 'Pegs team for offensive support. And, just before heading east to Toronto for their final two pre-Olympic exhibition games, the Winnipegs were given Norm Malloy of the Selkirks and Nels Crutchfield of McGill University. However, on the advice of his parents, Crutchfield declined the Olympic offer a few days later, leaving the Winnipegs with too little time to add a replacement. The team reinstated Clifford Crowley, whose place was to have been taken by Crutchfield.

The Winnipegs, 1932.

Canada-United States Feuding

Prior to and throughout these Games, the Americans did everything they could to bend the rules to their favour and distract the Canadians. Before arriving in Lake Placid, the U.S. team played a game against the Boston Bruins for which fans paid for their tickets, and the Olympic team pocketed a large portion of the receipts. "I am of the opinion that under the amateur rules the United States team has professionalized itself by playing against the Boston Bruins," said P.J. Mulqueen, chairman of the Canadian Olympic Committee. The Americans argued that without this revenue they could not afford to go to the Games, but the fact remained that they had contravened the then strict rules for amateurs.

Lou Marsh pointed out that team Canada could have done the same thing in Toronto, but it knew this would be a serious violation of the rules and so declined. He observed that, "You can bet your last centime that if the shoe was on the other foot—and the Canadian team had played a pro club for any object where a gate was taken—there would be a protest!!" After pointing out their misgivings about the Americans, however, the

Canada played most of its games outdoors (above) where conditions were less suited to their game than at the indoor venue (top).

Canadians, in true Conn Smythe spirit, refused to win a game off the ice and declined to launch a formal protest.

The Americans also frankly admitted to sending professional hockey players to the other two Olympics in which they competed, 1920 and 1924, again a basic violation of the prime tenet of the very existence of the Games. Stanley Woodward, in a column in the *New York Herald Tribune*, confessed: "As a matter of fact, our 1932 Olympic hockey team is a strictly amateur outfit... this is our first amateur Olympic hockey team." As one example, Irving Small, a member of the 1924 U.S. team, sued a hockey team shortly after those Games were over for what he claimed was back pay owed him for his play in an "amateur" hockey league! He was only one of many old pros to represent the United States in 1924.

Lastly, the village of Lake Placid featured two hockey venues, one outdoors and vastly inferior with a seating capacity of 8,000, the other in an arena with excellent ice but with a capacity less than half that. More specifically, the outdoor rink was contained inside the speed-skating oval! Spectators could see only half the rink and even then needed binoculars to distinguish players. The extreme cold did nothing to improve the spectator-appeal of the games. Despite the poor weather, horrible outdoor ice conditions, and extremely poor attendance (average of 1,500), most of the tournament was played outside, again to the detriment of quality of play.

The Canadians outscored their opponents 32-4 at the 1932 Olympics.

Team Canada's 1932 sweater featured a simple red maple leaf on the front.

1936 Garmisch–Partenkirchen, Germany

February 6–16, 1936

GOLD	Great Britain
Silver	CANADA
Bronze	United States
Fourth	Czechoslovakia
Fifth (tie)	Germany
	Sweden
Seventh (tie)	Austria, Hungary
Ninth (tie)	Italy, France
	Japan, Poland
Thirteenth (tie)	Belgium, Latvia
	Switzerland

TEAM CANADA: **Port Arthur Bear Cats**

Francis "Dinty" Moore, Arthur "Jakie" Nash, Walter "Pud" Kitchen, Ray Milton, Herman Murray (*captain*), Hugh Farquharson, Alexander Sinclair, Maxwell "Bill" Deacon, Ralph St. Germain, Dave Neville, Bill Thomson, Ken Farmer, Jim Haggarty, Norm Friday (*did not play*), Gus Saxberg (*did not play*), Al Pudas (*coach*), Malcolm Cochrane (*manager*)

The 1936 Port Arthur Bear Cats.

The Port Arthur Bear Cats

As was customary, the 1935 Allan Cup champions, the Halifax Wolverines, were selected to represent Canada at the 1936 Olympics. By late 1935, however, many of the players had moved away, were playing for different teams, or were no longer accessible. It became apparent that a reassembling of the team was impossible. The finalists for the Allan Cup that year, the Port Arthur Bear Cats, were thus regarded as the next best choice, and the CAHA asked them to represent Canada with the stipulation that players could be added if it felt such steps were necessary.

The Bear Cats spent much of January organizing their team, playing exhibition matches and figuring out which players would be needed to augment the team before sailing January 18 for Germany. They split a four-game series with the Fort William Wanderers in late 1935 and early 1936 before going to Toronto for more exhibition games against the Toronto Marlies. From there they moved on to Hamilton to play the Tigers, Brockville to play the Magedomas, and Kingston to play Queen's University. They followed with games in Montreal, Moncton, and Halifax before leaving for Garmisch–Partenkirchen.

Originally, the Bear Cats added eleven players to their training squad: Ralph St. Germain, Herman Murray, and Dave Neville from the Montreal Royals; Sylvester Bubar, Vic Ferguson, Chummy Lawlor, and Ernie Mosher from the Halifax Wolverines, Pud Kitchen of the Toronto Dukes, Hugh Farquharson of Montreal Victorias, Dinty Moore of the Port Colborne Sailors, and Jim Haggarty, formerly of the Bear Cats now playing for the Wembley Canadians in Britain.

Great Britain's gold-medal team from 1936.

Play around the Austrian goal during Canada's easy 5-2 win during the preliminary round.

The First Controversy... and Still in Canada

From the outset, this Olympics was fraught with unpleasant developments, changes in rules, dissatisfaction, and general chaos. It all began while the Bear Cats were in Toronto, and Canadian Olympic Committee president A.E. Gilroy received a demand from the four Halifax Wolverine players who had been added to the Bear Cats to help the team win the gold medal (Bubar, Ferguson, Lawlor, and Mosher). Incredibly, these four demanded "broken time" pay for their wives and families ($150 a month for three months), citing loss of income while they were away from home playing at the Olympics! Not only would this have tarnished the whole team's amateur status, it would have compromised the integrity of the team and the very reason for competing and defending Canada's honour as 1932 Olympic champions. These four were summarily dropped from the roster amid a chorus of Haligonian boos, leaving a much depleted but prouder team. They were immediately replaced by Kitchen, Farquharson, Moore, and Haggarty.

Game Conditions

Canada's first game of these Olympics was played outside, on frozen Lake Riessersee, under the worst conditions imaginable. Fewer than 300 fans braved a blinding snowstorm to see a game frequently stopped while the ice was cleared enough to permit proper skating or the puck searched for in among the snowbanks. At one point, the game was delayed several minutes before the puck was discovered under the foot of an attendant! At the same time, the Americans were playing inside, at the ice palace, before 8,000 comfortable patrons.

Tournament Format Decided Gold

Both the Germans and Canadians were enraged by what they felt was tantamount to cheating by the Olympic authorities who announced only after the second round was over that second-round matches would count in third round standings, thus overturning the original rules under which all teams were thought to have been playing. This virtually eliminated Canada from a gold medal on account of their second-round loss to Great Britain. Canadian official P.J. Mulqueen called it "one of the worst manipulations in sporting history," and *The Times* editorial agreed, saying euphemistically, "it is regrettable that the Olympic hockey committee didn't publicly announce the regulations governing the tournament."

Upon returning to native soil, however, most of the Canadian players placed responsibility for the format confusion on their own officials. Left winger Ralph St. Germain said plainly: "The Olympic rules state that the hockey may be played either on an elimination or point system or both. Either through carelessness or dumbness, the officials neglected to find out what system was being used until after we were defeated by England." Teammate Hugh Farquharson agreed: "No one realized, and the officials at least should have, that to lose that first game meant probable loss of the title. It would have made a big difference if that were known when we went into our game with England. That pool system has been in use over there for many years. There is no excuse for not completely understanding it before a Canadian team left Canada."

1948 St. Moritz, Switzerland

January 30–February 8, 1948

GOLD	CANADA
Silver	Czechoslovakia
Bronze	Switzerland
Fourth	Sweden
Fifth	Great Britain
Sixth	Poland
Seventh	Austria
Eighth	Italy

TEAM CANADA: Royal Canadian Air Force (RCAF) Flyers

Aircraftsman 2 Murray Dowey, Flying Officer Frank Dunster, Aircraftsman 2 André Laperrière, Flight Sergeant Louis Lecompte, Aircraftsman 1 Orval Gravelle, Corporal Patrick "Patsy" Guzzo, Wally Halder (*civilian*), Aircraftsman 1 Ted "Red" Hibberd, George Mara (*civilian, captain*), Leading Aircraftsman Ab Renaud, Flying Officer Reg Schroeter, Corporal Irving Taylor, Hubert Brooks (*did not play*), Roy Forbes (*did not play*), Andy Gilpin (*did not play*), Ross King (*did not play*), Pete Leichnitz (*did not play*), Sergeant Frank Boucher (*coach*), Squadron Leader A. Gardner "Sandy" Watson (*manager*)

The Royal Canadian Air Force (RCAF) Flyers

Despite Canada's supreme place in hockey, it was not until October 15, 1947, just 107 days before the first game of the 1948 Olympics was scheduled, that officials decided to send a team to represent the country. This waffling was based on a clear disagreement in defining "amateur" when the IIHF met in Zurich to prepare for the Games. Al Pickard, president of the CAHA, felt the rules were too strict, thus encouraging "under-the-table dealings" on the part of other countries, notably the United States, when trying to assemble a team of superior talent. In the end, it was felt that the greater injustice would have been not to participate at all, and the RCAF, who sported some of the finest "pure" amateurs in the country, volunteered their services. The CAHA gladly approved, and in their position as Canada's organizer vouched to pay for the players' expenses both to St. Moritz and while in training at the Auditorium in Ottawa (though costs towards the latter would be minimal as the players stayed at the Princess Alice Barracks on Argyle Street, right next door to the arena).

Putting the Team Together

Initial rumours had Red Dutton being named coach of the team, not only because of his long hockey record as player and president of the NHL, but also because he

The RCAF Flyers celebrate gold.

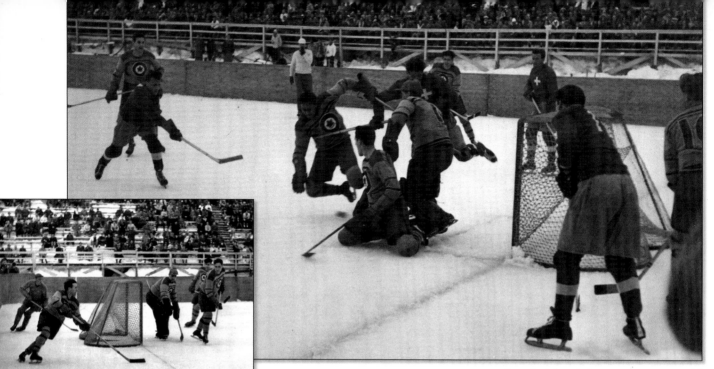

Goalie Murray Dowey watches his RCAF Flyers head up ice.

Canada defeated the Swiss 3-0 to win gold.

had lost both his sons in the war while they were serving with the RCAF. However, it was decided that Corporal Frank Boucher, coach of the RCAF team in the Ottawa City League, would be the more appropriate choice to cull talent from all stations across the country. Boucher had plenty of NHL experience (14 years) and also was a member of the RCAF overseas team that was highly regarded in amateur circles.

Boucher's father, George "Buck" Boucher, was put in charge of selecting and inviting troops to training camp. He acted as coach and decided on the final team in Ottawa while son Frank would take over full coaching duties in Switzerland. On October 19, the first players began arriving in Ottawa for tryouts, a process which eventually took much longer than expected. The first three were recruits from Winnipeg: F/L Jack Maitland, LAC Oscar Kleppe, and Sgt Lionel Bergeron. Three from the Toronto Station also arrived: F/L Bill McLeod, LAC Frank Hammond, and LAC Howard Kelly. Two players from Trenton were Sgt Nick Sargent and Sgt D. Sherman, and from Edmonton came F/O Bert Paxton. Arriving the next day were Del Sherman of Ottawa and Tom Moore of Montreal. Five new arrivals appeared October 29: AC1 Steve Chmara, AC1 Arthur Schultz, AC1 Arnold Metson, LAC Al Burgoin, and Roy Forbes.

By November 19, Boucher had the majority of the team selected, giving 13 players positions on the 17-man roster but only with the ever-present caveat, "if, before the team sails [January 8, 1948], other players prove of greater value, we will definitely make some changes."

The 13 were: defencemen Jack Seymour, Louis Lecompte, Stan Molinari, and Jack Maitland; forwards Orval Gravelle, Len Beatch, Irving Taylor, Hubert Brooks, Tommy Moore, Andy Gilpin, Roy Forbes, Dick Thomas, and Patrick Guzzo. Five days later, Trev Williams and Ross King were selected as goalies for the Canadians and three days before their first exhibition match, Louis Bergeron and George Wilson were included to fill the roster.

Canada's Games

The team played all of its games outdoors, and this caused havoc on a couple of occasions when snowstorms almost forced the cancellation of matches already under way. The refereeing was particularly European-partisan, and the penalties against Canada became a running joke for both team Canada and its opposition.

During the last two periods, when it became clear the Swiss were outclassed and on their way to losing, the crowd hurled snowballs at the Canadian skaters. The officiating was so biased it led the Flyers' trainer, Cpl George McFaul, to comment, "We played eight men—the Swiss players and the referees—and still beat 'em!"

Goalie Murray Dowey was also part of an interesting bit of Olympic trivia. Near the end of the team's first game, he caught the puck and threw it forward accidentally, a no-no in international hockey. Dowey was therefore given a two-minute penalty and had to go to the penalty box himself! Defenceman André Lapperrière took Dowey's stick and glove and played goal the last eight seconds of the game.

1952

Oslo, Norway
February 15–25, 1952

GOLD	CANADA
Silver	United States
Bronze	Sweden
Fourth	Czechoslovakia
Fifth	Switzerland
Sixth	Poland
Seventh	Finland
Eighth	West Germany
Ninth	Norway

TEAM CANADA: **Edmonton Mercurys**

Ralph Hansch, Eric Patterson, John Davies, Don Gauf, Bob Meyers, Tom Pollock, Al Purvis, George Abel, Billy Dawe (*captain*), Bruce Dickson, Billy Gibson, David Miller, Gordie Robertson, Louis Secco, Frank "Sully" Sullivan, Robert Watt, Lou Holmes (*coach*), Jim Christianson (*manager*)

The gold medalists from Edmonton pose for a team picture after returning home.

The Edmonton Mercurys

The Mercurys' selection by the CAHA to represent Canada at these Games differed slightly in rationale from the usual process of simply penning in the name of the Allan Cup champions. While teams from the west were still considered the best in Canada in 1951, the Western Senior A league had gone from being an amateur congregation in 1950 to semi-pro in 1951, thus disqualifying most of the teams and players from Olympic eligibility. The Mercurys,

an Intermediate club, were still highly regarded and through both their performance on ice and their clean record as amateurs they were invited to represent Canada in Oslo.

The Mercurys got to Europe early—by mid-December 1951—and stayed well after the Games were over, playing an extensive series of exhibition games throughout the Continent, at first to prepare themselves for the competition and then to promote their excellent skills and high standards of play and delight fans unused to seeing such a calibre of hockey.

This was the first time a Canadian team travelled to the Games by plane, leaving from Montreal and arriving at Prestwick, Scotland, on January 5, 1952. There, bedecked in white Stetsons, the Mercs were greeted by W. Duncan, president of the Scottish Ice Hockey Association, and Ross Low, manager of Ayr Arena. Less than an hour later, the Canadian boys were on the ice playing their first exhibition game, a 6–3 win over the Ayr Raiders. They played two more games in Scotland, then a series in London, and carried on to the Continent for more Olympic tune-ups.

The Guiding Light

The team was backed financially by Jim Christianson of Edmonton, a car dealer who provided the $100,000 needed to tour Europe and participate in the Olympics, and who, as owner, named the team after a brand of Fords he frequently sold. Christianson was in many ways a remarkable man and great hockey fan. He revived the Junior Oil Kings franchise which went on to win a Memorial Cup, and as owner of one of the most successful Lincoln Mercury dealerships in the country, his business acumen was indisputable.

While in Norway with the team, Christianson contracted a virus and was ill for most of the Games. Upon his return to Canada, he again became ill and died a short time later. The Ford Motor Company then appointed a dealer principal who oversaw operations for the next decade or so, and when he died, Mercs defenceman Al

Purvis was named the next dealer principal. Purvis then got a number of his Olympics teammates on board as shareholders (Miller, Gauf, and Dawe) or employees, each managing a division of the operations. Over the years, he bought back their shares, and to this day Al Purvis runs the Waterloo Mercury dealership in Edmonton, now celebrating more than 50 years of operation.

Mr. Zero—Ralph Hansch

Ralph Hansch is the answer to one of the more unique trivia questions about the history of Canadian hockey at the Olympics: Who is the only goalie to wear "0"? Having worn the number all through peewee and minors, Hansch saw no reason to alter his good luck number now that he had arrived at the biggest tournament of his life. The IOC frowned on the idea, however, and asked him to switch to a "real" number. He refused, but the IOC put a rule in its books making the future wearing of this digit illegal.

The Wrap-Up

After winning gold, the Mercurys travelled through Belgium, Holland, Sweden, Norway, Switzerland, Italy, and England again. All in all, they won 45 of the 50 games they played, the last a 7–2 win over the Earl's Court Rangers, before flying home April 1, 1952. They were greeted at the airport by Edmonton Mayor William Hawrelak, provincial government officials, wives, friends, fans, and well-wishers.

The Aftermath

Canada had been so far the superior hockey-playing nation in the world since 1920, and part of the teams' mandate had always been to tour Europe in good faith to promote hockey, Canada, and Canadian skills. In return, the players were culturally enriched by the time spent in these countries and they certainly enjoyed playing the games. However, they received no remuneration beyond living expenses (they were, after all, amateurs) and, worse, were frequently berated, most often during tense games at the Olympics, for incorporating too much the physical side of the game into play. This criticism exasperated the CAHA, which felt increasingly that travelling teams had little to gain and much to lose. Thus, the following year, the feeling was that Canada should not send a touring team to the World Championship in Switzerland, a decision made officially by CAHA president W.B. George but one fully supported by everybody.

Al Purvis's Olympic sweater.

1956 Cortina d'Ampezzo, Italy

January 26–February 4, 1956

GOLD	Soviet Union
Silver	United States
Bronze	CANADA
Fourth	Sweden
Fifth	Czechoslovakia
Sixth	Germany
Seventh	Italy
Eighth	Poland
Ninth	Switzerland
Tenth	Austria

TEAM CANADA: Kitchener-Waterloo Dutchmen

Denis Brodeur, Keith Woodall, Art Hurst, Byrle Klinck, Howie Lee, Jack MacKenzie (*captain*), Floyd Martin, Billy Colvin, Ken Laufman, Bob White, Charlie Brooker, Jim Logan, Don Rope, Gerry Theberge, Buddy Horne, Paul Knox, George Scholes, Bobby Bauer (*coach*), Ernie Gorman (*general manager*)

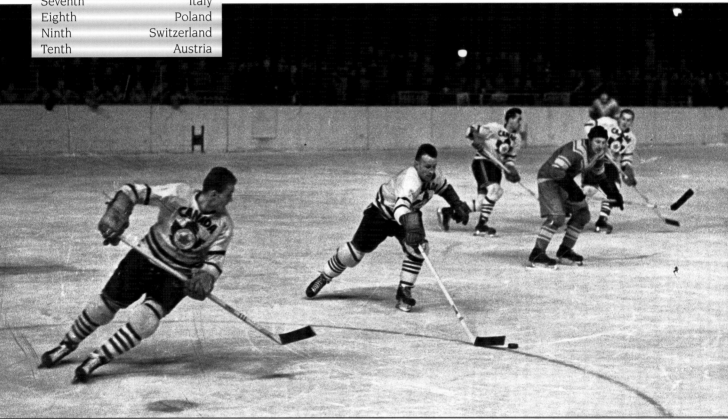

Canada's game against the Soviets was the highlight of 1956.

The Kitchener-Waterloo Dutchmen

The CAHA had an easy time selecting the Dutchmen as Canada's team for the 1956 Olympics, given that the K-Ws had won the Allan Cup the past two seasons. However, some replacements to the team that was competing in the five-team OHA Senior A would have to be made because of the amateur status required by Olympic rules. More specifically, Clare Martin, Bud Kemp, Joe Schertzel, Jack Hamilton, and Jack White were all professionals who had been reinstated for amateur play, which was fine for Senior OHA hockey, but not so fine for the Olympics.

To this end, the team signed forwards Bob White and Jim McBurney to replace the pros in November, and in early

January the Dutchmen further added Elmer Skov, George McLagan, and Art Hurst as possible final reinforcements for the Olympic tournament. Unfortunately, these were players from Senior B and Junior B teams, worth barely a whisper in Canada but at the time thought to be good enough for international competition. In retrospect, the addition of five higher-calibre players would probably have made a significant difference in the team's performance.

A further complication arose when it was decided that the Dutchmen would have to play the full OHA schedule if they were to qualify for the playoffs and defend their rule as Allan Cup champions. In the past, amateur teams and players had little problem getting

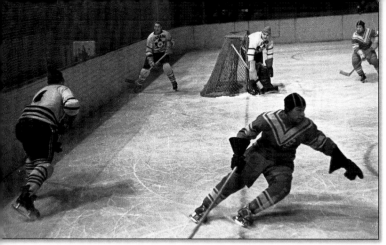

Action from Canada's 2-0 loss to the Soviets in the final game of 1956.

Goalie Keith Woodall watches defenceman Howie Lee handle the puck.

time off to ready themselves for the Olympics. For the Dutchies, representing Canada meant cramming many extra games before and after the Olympics into an even tighter time frame to meet league schedule requirements. At the start of December, for instance, they played five games in seven nights, a pace that would do nothing to improve the team's chances in Cortina.

The Referees

The 15 referees for the Olympics threatened to quit the Games just prior to their opening, citing poor accommodations and an IOC failure to reimburse them for out-of-pocket expenses. Once this problem was straightened out, the skill and competence of European officials was questioned. It was brought to the attention of Bunny Ahearne, European president of the IIHF, who then proposed ways of overcoming the poor skating ability of the Continental zebras.

Ahearne wanted to put the refs in some sort of cage that would be elevated above the ice, so they could make the calls from an easier vantage point and not have to skate all the while. He explained: "A spotlight would follow the referee up and down the rope ladder [leading to the cage], thus giving the fans a chance to blow off steam. The ice would be marked off into numbered areas for faceoffs and the referee would announce over the loudspeaker the reason for penalties. One or two linesmen would be on the ice simply to handle faceoffs and get between fighters." The idea, thankfully, never took hold.

The Aftermath of Losing: Assessing the Damage

For Canada, the team didn't win a bronze medal as much as it lost a gold. The result was considered a dismal failure. It was the worst placing a Canadian team had achieved in 36 years of Olympic hockey. The result, however, was not without some benefit, signalling a new era in Olympic competition and a significant skewing of the amateur-professional dichotomy.

Soviet official Roman Kiselev was asked how much professional hockey players were paid in the USSR. His answer: "There are no professionals in Russia." So, while the Soviets operated a league of their own and trained their Olympians eight months or more of the year, apparently none of them actually made a ruble directly or indirectly. When asked who would win if the Soviets played Canada's best players—Howe, Richard et al.—Kiselev was equally terse, saying only that "Richard and Howe are not here [at the Olympics]."

By the same token, the Canadians in charge of the country's Olympic representatives were again questioning the team concept, suggesting again that an all-star team format would be better, if not essential, if Canada were to remain competitive in the years ahead, especially if the Soviets were going to continue to send "non-professional" professionals to the Games and World Championships each time. Nor was it just the assemblage of the team that was of concern. The Russians prepared intensely for these two events year-round; the Canadians forced a club team to play a demanding schedule in league play right before the Games and expected the team to walk away with the gold.

Those days were at an end.

1960

Squaw Valley, California

February 19–28, 1960

GOLD	United States
Silver	CANADA
Bronze	Soviet Union
Fourth	Czechoslovakia
Fifth	Sweden
Sixth	Germany
Seventh	Finland
Eighth	Japan
Ninth	Australia

TEAM CANADA: Kitchener–Waterloo Dutchmen

Don Head, Harold "Boat" Hurley, Moe Benoit, Jack Douglas, Harry Sinden (*captain*), Darryl Sly, Bob Attersley, Jim Connelly, Fred Etcher, Bob Forhan, Ken Laufman, Floyd "Butch" Martin, Bob McKnight, Cliff Pennington, Don Rope, Bobby Rousseau, George Samolenko, Bobby Bauer (*coach*), Ernie Gorman (*general manager*)

The Return of the Kitchener-Waterloo Dutchmen

The 1959 Allan Cup champion Whitby Dunlops declined the invitation to represent Canada at Squaw Valley, thus paving the way for the Dutchies to appear in their second successive Olympics. As in 1956, they were at a disadvantage right away, losing three of their top players—Bill Kennedy, George Gosselin, and Dick Mattiussi—to the pros.

Furthermore, the team was once again in the Senior OHA loop, meaning they had to finish off a gruelling 48-game schedule before leaving on a one-month exhibition tour on their way to Squaw Valley. This time, the other Senior A teams promised to help in any way they could as far as replacement players were concerned, provided they received replacements themselves and $500 per man loaned. To this end, the Dutchies got Bob Attersley, Fred Etcher, George Samolenko, and Harry Sinden from the Dunlops, Moe Benoit from the Belleville MacFarlands, Don Head from the Windsor Bulldogs, and Jack and Jim Connelly from the Chatham Maroons. The Montreal Canadiens also made Bobby Rousseau available for the team.

To help the Dutchies financially, the twin cities of Kitchener–Waterloo established a committee to raise $17,000 for the team's expenses, including travel, doctors,

The Americans defeated the Soviets 3-2 in the final round of play.

Goalie Jack McCartan.

trainers, extra baggage, and insurance. The money was raised through a $2,000 donation from Conn Smythe, $1,000 from the Canadiens, and $12,000 through ticket sales for a car that was to be auctioned off.

K-W Coaching

Although the record books show Bobby Bauer coached this 1960 entry, he was by no means the man intended to be there. The Dutchies already had a coach the year before and at the start of this season, former Canadiens great Bill Durnan, but he quit the team after a six-game losing streak, forcing the Dutchies to find a replacement. Initially it was to have been Joe Primeau, then Ted Kennedy, then Happy Day, but none of these well-known ex-Leafs could get the

time off necessary to prepare for the demanding task that lay ahead. They had all been out of hockey awhile and had successful business interests they wanted to nurture and could not afford time off for the sake of such a short-term commitment. It was then that Bauer agreed to the challenge, despite the caustic, pessimistic words of NHL president Clarence Campbell, who declared that, "Canada's Olympic entry does not have the best management and coaching, which is needed if the team is to win."

The team left Kitchener-Waterloo on January 31, 1960 by chartered bus, using the drive west to squeeze in a two-week Western Canadian exhibition tour. They won all seven games they played before arriving in Squaw Valley just a few days prior to their first Olympic game.

Looking Ahead to Major Change

For the second Olympics in a row, the Canadians lost a game to the Americans and also failed to win the gold medal. This was indicative of two factors, both of which would have to be addressed if Canada were ever to remain atop the international hockey heap. First, the idea of taking a single club to represent the country no longer seemed possible. After all, this K–W team, an excellent amateur team, had, in the end, only eight original members on the final Olympic roster. Thus, the whole concept of choosing a team—because the players knew each other and had played together for a long time—was thrown out the window. Rather than do things by halves, it was time to select the team player by player rather than attempt to fill huge gaps in one team's lineup. There were many highly skilled juniors and amateurs who weren't playing in the Games, partly because of the team concept, but mostly because the finest amateurs were quickly signed to pro contracts by the Big Six NHL teams.

Furthermore, the players competing for communist countries, most notably the USSR, were the 17 best players in that country. It is without any question that if the finest 17 Canadians in 1960—Gordie Howe, Terry Sawchuk, Henri Richard, George Armstrong, Jean Beliveau et al.— were permitted to represent Canada, they would have won the gold medal almost uncontested. However, the Olympic association was not bending on its amateur rule, so Canada clearly had to adapt to change by ensuring that for the 1964 Games the finest 20 hockey players in the country not signed to pro contracts represented Canada. Bobby Bauer was a respected, capable coach; the Kitchener–Waterloo Dutchmen had been Allan Cup champions twice; yet, the team neither represented Canada's best amateurs nor won the gold medal.

1964 Innsbruck, Austria

January 29–February 9, 1964

GOLD	Soviet Union	Ninth	Poland	
Silver	Sweden	Tenth	Norway	
Bronze	Czechoslovakia	Eleventh	Japan	
Fourth	CANADA	Twelfth	Romania	
Fifth	United States	Thirteenth	Austria	
Sixth	Finland	Fourteenth	Yugoslavia	
Seventh	Germany	Fifteenth	Italy	
Eighth	Switzerland	Sixteenth	Hungary	

TEAM CANADA: **National Team**

Ken Broderick, Seth Martin, Hank Akervall (*captain*), Barry MacKenzie, Terry O'Malley, Rod Seiling, Gary Begg, Gary Dineen, George Swarbrick, Roger Bourbonnais, Terry Clancy, Brian Conacher, Ray Cadieux, Paul Conlin, Bob Forhan, Marshall Johnston, Father David Bauer (*coach*), Dr. Bob Hindmarch (*manager*)

The Dawn of a New Era

Taking Gordon Juckes' 1960 report to heart, Father David Bauer had become increasingly concerned by Canada's poor showing in international competitions and equally aware that the country's top amateur teams were no longer the cream of the crop, the absolute favourites, the shoe-in gold medallists. Bauer was also very confident that academics and athletics could make successful bedfellows

Father Bauer and his players pose for a unique team photo.

Marshall Johnston's 1964 Olympic sweater.

After the game, IIHF president Bunny Ahearne suspended Oberg for one game for deliberately trying to injure Canada's coach. As well, the Swiss referee who failed to give Oberg a penalty on the play was also suspended for a game. In an expression of sportsmanship and forgiveness, Father Bauer invited Oberg to be his guest the next night to watch the Czechoslovakia–USSR game, a gesture that earned international acclaim for its kindness and sporting understanding.

That night, the two sat side by side at the Ice Stadium where the Canadians were given a huge cheer from the 11,000 fans. At the end of the Olympics, Father Bauer was awarded a special gold medal for "the control he exercised over his players" during the stick throwing incident which easily could have turned into a full-scale brawl.

and that university students were just as capable of winning gold as any Soviet congregation of talent. In June 1962, when the CAHA held its summer meetings in Toronto, Father Bauer proposed a system whereby the top amateurs in university and Senior A could play together for close to a year in preparation for major tournaments, specifically the Olympics and World Championships.

With little fanfare and plenty of confidence, Father Bauer officially began his term as Canada's National Team coach on August 21, 1963, when players gathered at UBC to begin training for the 1964 Olympics. This was Father Bauer's vision, his solution to the problems of assembling a truly amateur team, one that was both national and of the highest calibre. He invited the best amateurs to a training camp that would be maintained for the better part of half a year. No last-minute additions, no exhausted league team representation, no weak links. The team would practise together and tour together before heading to Innsbruck for the Olympics. The plan may not have been perfect, but the status quo was clearly the least desirable option. Change of any sort seemed progressive.

Father Bauer's Gesture

During play in the Canada–Sweden game at the Olympics, Carl Oberg, a Swedish forward, threw his broken stick into the Canadian bench as he skated to his own bench to get a new one. The stick hit an unsuspecting coach Bauer in the forehead, causing a cut to open. The Canadian players were furious, and were ready to defend their honour by pummelling Oberg and his team to full extent, but Bauer restrained his corps and pleaded for calmness.

Loss to the Czechs

Canada's final two games of the tournament were against their toughest opponents, Czechoslovakia and the Soviet Union. In the Czech game, and in fact throughout the Olympics, Canada's Seth Martin was brilliant in goal, and with fewer than ten minutes remaining, his team still had a slim 1–0 lead thanks to Rod Seiling's second-period goal. However, on one enemy rush, a Czech player collided with Martin, who fell clutching his left leg. Injured but determined, Martin tried to continue, but two minutes later he had to come out of the net. Ken Broderick took his place, but with no warm-up and almost no Olympic experience he was at a serious disadvantage. The Canadians could not protect him, and Broderick was not as hot as Martin had been. The Czechs put three goals into the Canadian net in just eight minutes to win the game and deflate Canada's hopes for gold. They fought valiantly but lost the next game too, 3–2, to the Soviets.

The Players and the Pontiff

As a man of the cloth, Father Bauer had as much influence off the ice as he did on it as coach. Following the disappointment of the Games, the National Team played two exhibitions against Canadian Armed Forces teams stationed in West Germany and then travelled to Rome. Although it was winter in Canada and Austria, it was balmy in Italy, and the Canadians looked their part walking down the Via Condotti in their heavy Hudson Bay parkas! Father Bauer took the players to Vatican City where the Swiss Guards outside St. Peter's wanted to know which one was "Seeth," Canada's famous goalie, Seth Martin! Martin had become a legend in Europe after his play in the World Championships in 1961 and again in 1963, and was by far the most identifiable member of the team.

1968 Grenoble, France

February 6–17, 1968

GOLD	Soviet Union	Eighth	East Germany
Silver	Czechoslovakia	Ninth	Yugoslavia
Bronze	CANADA	Tenth	Japan
Fourth	Sweden	Eleventh	Norway
Fifth	Finland	Twelfth	Romania
Sixth	United States	Thirteenth	Austria
Seventh	West Germany	Fourteenth	France

TEAM CANADA: **National Team**

Ken Broderick, Wayne Stephenson, Paul Conlin, Brian Glennie, Ted Hargreaves, Marshall Johnston (*captain*), Barry MacKenzie, Terry O'Malley, Roger Bourbonnais, Ray Cadieux, Gary Dineen, Fran Huck, Billy MacMillan, Steve Monteith, Morris Mott, Danny O'Shea, Gerry Pinder, Herb Pinder, Jackie McLeod (*coach*), Father David Bauer (*manager*)

Canada's Preparation: Father Bauer's Program Continues Apace

The dream that started in 1963 when Father Bauer established a national junior squad had now become part of Canada's yearly hockey operations, and the preparation for the 1968 Olympics began for Canada earlier than ever before when the players hit the ice at Dutton Arena at St. John's–Ravenscourt School in Fort Garry, Manitoba, on August 9, 1967, fully six months before their first Olympic game.

The first few days of camp featured mostly newcomers and hopefuls, rookies who were eager to make an impression with coach MacLeod early, a chance they would be given just a week later when the Nats faced a team of NHL All-Stars, including rookie-of-the-year Bobby Orr, and league veterans Carl Brewer, Ab McDonald, and Pete Stemkowski, in a charity match. In a new twist, the National Team would also play as two teams for a number of months at varying tournaments, one playing out of Winnipeg in the Western Canadian Senior League, and the other, based in Ottawa, playing in the Quebec Provincial Senior League under alumnus Jack Bownass. This, coach MacLeod felt, would give the greatest number of players the greatest opportunity to show their skills and prove themselves worthy of the final Olympic roster. At the same time, though, it divided the team and prevented the final squad from using this time to get to know one another on ice, thus creating a situation similar to previous years when the final team—the actual players who would go to the Olympics—weren't put together soon enough or for long enough.

Orr's appearance in Manitoba for the benefit game created a remarkable stir, but, ominously, he played just eight minutes before suffering a knee injury that kept him

The Soviets beat Canada 5-0 during the Olympics to win gold and force the young Canadian team to go home with a bronze medal.

Goalie Ken Broderick faces a shot during an exhibition game against the Soviets in preparation for the 1968 Olympics in Grenoble.

off ice until the start of the Bruins' training camp some three weeks later. To augment their games in the Western Senior League, which wouldn't provide a particularly stiff challenge for the Olympians, the team also played a number of tougher exhibition games in the coming months against the US Nationals, the Eastern Nationals, and a selection of NHL teams, and also partook in another pre-Olympic tournament in Prague.

USSR 5 – Canada 0

More than 15,000 people packed the Stade de Glace in Grenoble to see this gold medal game. The vast majority were chanting, "Canada! Canada!" The outcome of this match could be put in the simplest terms: a win meant a gold medal, a tie meant a silver, a loss meant a bronze.

While both teams maintained a blistering pace and hit fiercely and cleanly, the Soviets got the upper hand on a Canadian power play. Anatoly Firsov's first period, short-handed goal gave the Russians a 1–0 lead that held up until midway through the second period.

All along, it was the Canadians' ability to score, to finish their plays, that had been questioned, and no greater example of this weakness can be cited than the second period. The flip side to the argument, of course, is that the Russians got great goaltending. Either way, Russian gaoler Viktor Konovalenko stopped Fran Huck close in and then Mott and Pinder in quick succession. Michakov went in alone on Ken Broderick on the counter-attack, and the USSR was up 2–0. The Redshirts followed with a goal early in the third to leave no doubt of the outcome, and two later goals the loss was affirmed.

The Post-mortem

While a medal, albeit bronze, might have gone over well with just about any other hockey playing nation, it was a portentous achievement, to say the least, for Canada. After the Olympics, critics were fighting each other to be at the front of the coach-bashing line, not necessarily knocking Jackie McLeod in particular, but rather heaping praise on Russian leader Anatoly Tarasov as a man far more sage and erudite than his Canadian counterparts. They talked about how the Russians were on the ice every day, ten months of the year, for five hours, practising every possible skill needed to win.

Canada was at a crossroads: to keep sending under-qualified players to the Games in the name of competition, amateur fair play, dedication, and upholding the Olympic ideal, or to do something drastic to voice a collective frustration and displeasure at not being allowed to use professionals Canada chose the latter. Either pros would represent the country in upcoming Olympics and World Championships, or Canada would not send a hockey team to international events.

1972–1976

Canada Withdraws from International Competition

Establishing Hockey Canada

As a result of winning the 1968 federal election, Prime Minister Pierre Trudeau fulfilled a campaign promise by commissioning a Task Force on Sports aimed at understanding amateur hockey in Canada and why its programs had become increasingly unsuccessful in the past decade. The committee concluded that one organizing body should be created to oversee all levels of amateur hockey and control all necessary plans for national and international competitions. To this end, Hockey Canada Inc. was formed on February 24, 1969. A charitable organization that comprised the CAHA, CIAU, Fitness and Amateur Sport, and the NHL's two Canadian teams, the Leafs and Canadiens, its mandate was as complex as its wording was simple: "To support, operate, manage, and develop a national team or teams for the purpose of representing Canadian international tournaments and competitions. To foster and support the playing of hockey in Canada and in particular the development of the skill and competence of Canadian hockey players and, in this connection, to cooperate with other bodies, groups and associations having similar or related purposes and objectives."

Initially, though, Hockey Canada felt that since Canada was being awarded host country honours for the World Championships in 1970 for the first time (to be co-hosted by Winnipeg and Montreal), its goal should be to make it an open competition, one in which Canada's professionals could compete. When the IIHF met at Crans-sur-Sierre, Switzerland in July 1969, the question of professional participation headed the agenda, both because of Canada's discontent with the current set-up and our status as host nation for the 1970 Worlds. The IIHF agreed to allow nine non-NHL pros into each tournament for one year, after which a full review would decide the long-term future of the practice (the theory being that if some pros were allowed to play, Canada would be mollified, but that NHLers were of too high a calibre for the Europeans' liking). It wasn't all Hockey Canada had hoped for, but organizers were optimistic nonetheless.

The first significant test for the rule was the Izvestia tournament in Moscow at Christmas 1969. Canada used only five pros and finished a close second, and as a result the IIHF held an emergency meeting on January 3, 1970 immediately after the tournament's conclusion. At this time, president Avery Brundage did an about-face and announced that any players competing with Canada's pros in the future would be forfeiting their amateur status and would not be eligible to compete at the Olympics. Hockey Canada members were red with rage.

Since its participation in competition in 1956, the Soviets had dominated world tournaments because, not to mince words, they used pros. In Canada, the term routinely coined was "shamateurs," for the Olympics was becoming an ethical farce, on the one hand staunchly upholding ideals of sportsmanship, fair play, and clean competition, on the other allowing professionals from communist countries to participate.

In response to the IIHF's decision to force Canada's hand and rescind the earlier "nine pros" agreement, Earl Dawson, president of the CAHA, declared point blank that if the non-NHL pros were not given full international sanctions, Canada would not host the Worlds, would withdraw from international competition altogether, and would not send teams on goodwill exhibition tours through Europe in the future.

At a meeting in Geneva shortly after this announcement, Dawson seemed also to have come up with a favourable counter-proposal: the World Championships would be scrapped and replaced with an invitational series featuring five teams. No medals would be awarded, and Canada could field any team it wanted without jeopardizing the Olympic status of anyone from any of the five countries—Canada, USSR, Czechoslovakia, Finland, and Sweden. While the other countries ruminated over the idea, Brundage made clear his belief that this would compromise the players' Olympic eligibility. The other teams quickly backed away from the idea, and Canada made the proud and correct choice—it followed through on its threat and withdrew from all international competitions, except the Olympics.

Dawson explained: "Canada will enter a team of amateurs in the 1972 Olympic Games and we intend to question the eligibility of every other team and make ineligible any and all teams which have played professionally."

Reaction in Canada to the decision was swift, unanimous, and fully supportive. John Munro, federal minister of national health and welfare, was first in line to praise those who made the tough decision: "Our country has not been able to ice the best teams because of farcical regulations which made it impossible to use players with the same experience as those other countries used. Canada has some pride."

Meanwhile, players with the other countries weren't really as concerned over their Olympic status as they were about implementing any rule change that helped Canada. Russia feared the nine Canadian pros would be enough to end their seven-year hold on the World Championships; Sweden became host now that Canada withdrew, thus giving their team a better chance of winning; East Germany and Czechoslovakia would do nothing to offend Mother Russia.

Despite the huge support for the decision, one very serious question remained. Regardless of the medal results at all these Soviet-won Games, the experience of playing international hockey was absolutely invaluable for young Canadian players. Without such experience, how could Canada hope to keep producing top-notch players? And what about Hockey Canada, an organization swamped with young men who learned and grew through international participation? Was it not still honourable to compete and play by the rules, even if no one else did? In a special report for the *Telegram*, former Leaf coach Punch Imlach wrote: "The national team has come a long way and it would be folly to discontinue operations just because the [world] tournament has been changed… I have always thought that the stronger the amateur leagues, the stronger the professionals. A good foundation is always good business."

The conflict, then, was twofold. On the one hand, any time a country competes in a tournament, it wants to win. Canada would certainly have won all the Olympics had NHLers played. On the other hand though, since Canada couldn't use pros, should it still compete for the sake of the experience, even knowing the team probably wasn't going to win? The problem was that despite competing, Canada's international reputation was taking a battering and the country's hockey morale was slipping. Canada now seemed second-best to the Soviet Union because it kept placing second in tournaments. Canada's amateurs were still phenomenal athletes at a world level, among the best, but clearly not the best. The time had come to compete one-on-one, our best versus their best, winner take all—accolades, bragging rights, and rankings.

The Summit Series

After beating Canada 5–0 in the 1968 Olympics, Soviet coach Anatoly Tarasov defiantly boasted that his team could beat any in the NHL. Soon he would get his chance to prove it. Hockey Canada, through sublime negotiations, led by NHL Players' Association president and player agent Alan Eagleson, arranged an eight-game tournament with the Russians, the very best players in Canada against any team that the Soviets could put together. The first four games would be played in Canada, the last four in Moscow. The dates were September 1–28, 1972.

The player selections for the two teams told a story in itself. The Russians had 13 players who had played at the Sapporo Winter Olympics earlier in the year and, incredibly, seven men who had played against Canada at the 1968 Winter Olympics at Grenoble. Team Canada had not one player for the Summit Series who had any international experience, fully indicating Canada had never had the chance to play its best at the world level while confirming that Russia used only its best at all times.

The series proved a defining moment in Canada's cultural and sporting history, easily the most remarkable example of the bond between national identity and sport uniting Canada from coast to coast. Down 3–1 in games with one tie, the Canadians had to win the last three matches, all in Russia, if they were to win the series and prove themselves the best, to erase the years of accusations of cheating and fraud they had hurled at the Russians each Olympics and World Championships.

Today, Canadians over 40 recall vividly where they were on September 28, 1972 when Foster Hewitt screamed across the nation's television sets that "Henderson has scored for Canada!" This remarkable Summit—called the Summit Series—proved a number of things: Canada had better players, and many more of them, than Russia; Russia's "pro" team was the same as their "amateur" team; and the gap between them and us wasn't as great as we had thought. Canadian pride, integrity, fortitude, desire, and heart won the series and established a reputation that has won this country many, many games and medals over the years.

1980 Lake Placid, New York

February 13–24, 1980

GOLD	United States
Silver	Soviet Union
Bronze	Sweden
Fourth	Finland
Fifth	Czechoslovakia
Sixth	CANADA
Seventh	Poland
Eighth	Romania
Ninth (tie)	Holland
	Norway
Eleventh (tie)	West Germany
	Yugoslavia
Thirteenth	Japan

TEAM CANADA: National Team

Bob Dupuis, Paul Pageau, Warren Anderson, Joe Grant, Randy Gregg (*captain*), Terry O'Malley, Brad Pirie, Don Spring, Tim Watters, Glenn Anderson, Ken Berry, Dan D'Alvise, Ron Davidson, John Devaney, Dave Hindmarch, Paul MacLean, Kevin Maxwell, Jim Nill, Kevin Primeau, Stelio Zupancich, Doug Buchanan (*did not play*), Cary Farelli (*did not play*), Roger Lamoureux (*did not play*), Ron Paterson (*did not play*), Shane Pearsall (*did not play*), Lorne Davis (*co-coach*), Clare Drake (*co-coach*), Tom Watt (*co-coach*), Rick Noonan (*manager*), Father David Bauer (*managing director*)

The Hockey Program Reborn

Although Father David Bauer's dream of a national junior team came to fruition between 1963 and 1969, Canada's withdrawal from international hockey pretty much ended the need for the concept. However, with Canada's return to the World Championship in 1977 and the Olympics in 1980, Father Bauer was able to convince Hockey Canada to reinstitute his idea of one team that trained together for a full season. The argument was still sound and since there was none better, training camp opened in Calgary in August 1979 to full national support.

As before, players came mostly from Canadian universities, which was why Father Bauer selected coaches Tom Watt (University of Toronto) and Clare Drake

American captain Mike Eruzione battles for position with Soviet Valeri Vasiliev.

The Canada-USSR Showdown

As usual, this game would almost certainly decide the gold medal. Despite being heavy underdogs, a team of university students going up against one that had been playing half a dozen years or more together (seven players in this lineup had been on the 1972 Summit Series team), the proud Canadians almost stole a victory. It wasn't until midway through the third that the Soviets gained a lead they didn't relinquish.

While both teams stood at their respective blue lines for the playing of the Russian national anthem after the Soviet victory, it was that Canada received a standing ovation from the supportive fans for their incredible fight, collegians playing stride for stride with the best Russia could offer. What was the difference in talent? These were the best players in the whole Soviet Union, while of the 20 members of the Canadian team, only nine had played more than two games in the NHL!

The National Hockey Dream Revived

While the Canadians may have lost on the scoreboard to the Russians that final afternoon in Lake Placid, they won the emotional battle and were so impressive that the result could almost be said to have kept Father Bauer's national program alive. "I think our objectives have been partially realized," he concluded, "but we have to hope that playing for their country doesn't obscure the other values to be derived from this experience. The whole rationale was to provide another option wherein some form of education could be involved, wherein some experiences other than hockey might be a part of human growth. These fellows have received pretty good coaching; they've improved their skills; hopefully this experience broadened their horizons. I think the game against the Russians brought all of these together."

Lou Lefaive, president of Hockey Canada, was equally buoyed by the results: "There's no question that the [national team] concept is one that we're going to keep alive and we'll try to keep as many of these players as we can. We're taking them to a tournament in Sweden in April almost as a unit… we'll try to bring this team together, as many of them that we can, for the Pravda tournament, for the Izvestia tournament, and we'll be gearing towards next year's World Championship in Sweden." The concept of a national dream was still, however, very much a compromise between only competing and doing everything possible to win. Canada was allowed to have pros at the World Championships (governed by the IIHF) as compensation for guaranteeing a commitment to the Olympics without pros (governed by the IOC).

Goalie Jim Craig makes one of several great saves against the Soviets.

(University of Alberta) to select the camp roster. Between them, Watt and Drake had won eleven of the previous 12 national titles, an achievement which certainly attested to their abilities to work with young players and their thorough knowledge of the CIAU (Canadian Intrauniversity Athletic Union). In certain cases, Watt and Drake also added Canadian players at American colleges on scholarships, and those playing in other countries.

The players lived in the "Rig," portable dormitories donated by an oil company that had used them previously at a drilling site in Alaska, and they practised at the Calgary Corral. The team participated in the challenging Rudi Pravo tournament in Prague in September, played six games against NHL clubs (losing only to Washington and the Rangers), won four of six exhibitions against the American national team, and then hosted a series of matches against the Moscow Dynamo, the Czech "B" team, and colleges across North America. In December, the team was divided into two groups, one heading for the Izvestia tournament in Moscow, the other to an important pre-Olympic tournament in Lake Placid.

1984

Sarajevo, Yugoslavia
February 7–19, 1984

GOLD	Soviet Union
Silver	Czechoslovakia
Bronze	Sweden
Fourth	CANADA
Fifth	West Germany
Sixth	Finland
Seventh	United States
Eighth	Poland
Ninth	Italy
Tenth	Norway
Eleventh (tie)	Austria
	Yugoslavia

TEAM CANADA: **National Team**

Darren Eliot, Mario Gosselin, Warren Anderson, Robin Bartel, J.J. Daigneault, Bruce Driver, Doug Lidster, James Patrick, Craig Redmond, Russ Courtnall, Kevin Dineen, Dave Donnelly, Pat Flatley, Dave Gagner, Vaughn Karpan, Darren Lowe, Kirk Muller, Dave Tippett (*captain*), Carey Wilson, Dan Wood, Dave King (*coach & general manager*), George Kingston (*assistant coach*), Jean Perron (*assistant coach*)

Putting Team Canada 1984 Together

The ideal situation for coach Dave King and his staff heading towards the 1984 Games would have mirrored that of virtually every other coach since Canada and hockey began at the Olympics in 1920: select a team, keep it training together for six months, and enter the Games as the most skilled group of amateurs in the country. However, the roster that appeared at the training camp in August 1983 to prepare for the Games and the one that King listed on the official score sheet for the first Olympic game were vastly different, thanks to the addition of new players (Kirk Muller and Russ Courtnall, for instance), injuries (Joe Grant, Gord Sherven and George Servinis), and the inevitable international squabble over who was amateur and who professional.

One player who was caught between the national team and the NHL was Michel Petit of the Vancouver Canucks. Originally, the Canucks had agreed to loan Petit to the Nats until the Olympics were over, then have him rejoin the NHL team in February '84. However, NHL rules stated that a junior could not be promoted to the NHL after January 1 of any season unless there were an injury on the parent club. In other words, if Petit were to join Team Canada in September '83, he couldn't count on playing for the Canucks until September '84. The Canucks thought too highly of their prospect to lose him for that long, and so, after starting the year with the Olympians (joining the team October 6), Petit was recalled before the year was out and never made the Sarajevo sojourn.

A similar controversy on a smaller scale unfolded in the form of J.J. Daigneault, the only junior on the team, who was playing for Longueuil in the QMJHL. Longueuil contended he was under contract to the club and couldn't simply join the national team without permission, which he did anyway. It took a bit of negotiating and legal wrangling, but he was finally able to remain with Dave King after getting Longueuil's permission. Daigneault was becoming part of an evermore active group of young players who craved the international experience, both for the culture of the sport and as a means of being exposed to a higher calibre of competition.

A year later, Team Canada '84 teammate Pat Flatley would look back and call his decision to play "the best thing I ever did," citing the huge improvements he had made in his game under the tutelage of King. "I developed quickness, which I didn't have before. The Olympic coaches taught me techniques for getting into open ice—again, something you really need in the NHL… I didn't have the remotest idea about playing in the neutral zone. For that matter, I didn't know much about defensive hockey at all. But by the time the Olympics were over, I'd received a very thorough education."

After the Olympics—The NHL

After the Olympics ended and Canada's fourth place finish was in the books, the team travelled to Paris for exhibition games against the Soviet and Czech "B" teams, as well as a West German team, before heading home and disbanding. The next stop for Team Canada was the 1984 Canada Cup. Not surprisingly, the country's best beat everyone else's best—again. One player, James Patrick, played for both the Olympic team and Canada Cup team for Canada in 1984. Incredibly, fully 18 members of the 1984 Russian Olympic team also played in the Canada Cup. Of the Canadian Olympians, each and every member to play at the 1984 Games went on to play in the NHL.

While the Canada Cup victory boosted the country's morale (the team was made up entirely of NHLers), the national hockey program as a whole was still, as ever, in flux. If a national amateur program were to stay in place for the next four years, it would need strong international competition, but this was impossible when the pros now dominated the World Championships roster and the Juniors at the World Junior Championships had Major Junior A affiliation in Canada (thus restricting their international eligibility). The current national program was the best at nurturing that talent, but it risked becoming an isolated junior team with no place to play. Yet the pros showed no signs of closing down the NHL for the 1988 Games at Calgary, thus placing the future of an Olympic medal squarely on the amateur program.

Bruce Driver's sweater from 1984.

1984, Sarajevo, Yugoslavia

1988 Calgary, Alberta
February 13–28, 1988

GOLD	Soviet Union
Silver	Finland
Bronze	Sweden
Fourth	CANADA
Fifth	West Germany
Sixth	Czechoslovakia
Seventh	United States
Eighth	Switzerland
Ninth	Austria
Tenth	Poland
Eleventh	France
Twelfth	Norway

TEAM CANADA

Sean Burke, Andy Moog, Chris Felix, Randy Gregg, Serge Roy, Tony Stiles, Tim Watters, Trent Yawney, Zarley Zalapski, Ken Berry, Mark Habscheid, Vaughn Karpan, Wally Schreiber, Gord Sherven, Claude Vilgrain, Serge Boisvert, Brian Bradley, Bob Joyce, Merlin Malinowski, Jim Peplinski, Steve Tambellini, Ken Yaremchuk, Rick Kosti (*did not play*), Dave King (*coach & general manager*), Guy Charron (*assistant coach*), Tom Watt (*assistant coach*)

Slava Fetisov's 1988 Olympic sweater.

The Professionals are Coming to Town

As early as October 20, 1986, IIHF president Gunther Sabetzki announced that any and all pros—no restrictions on age, numbers, or leagues—would be able to participate in the 1988 Olympics, making Calgary the first truly "open" Games for hockey. "There are no restrictions," Sabetzki declared. "Canada can use Wayne Gretzky if it wants to." NHL president John Zeigler, however, made it clear that what Canada wanted and what it got were two different things: "We put on a thousand events a year. Most of our sales are season tickets. I don't think it's fair to the customer if we say, 'You've paid $16 for your ticket—oh, by the way, for the next three weeks you're not going to see the Gretzkys, the Paul Coffeys, and the Bourques and so forth.' What would that do to the integrity of the competition?" Alas, the great opportunity put on the international table by Sabetzki had no takers.

While NHL players had been allowed to compete in the World Championships since 1977 (sanctioned by the IIHF), this was the first time they were allowed to play at the Olympics (sanctioned by the IOC). So, although the results were not remarkable—no NHL team actually allowed a top-notch star to leave—it did set the tone for 1998 in Nagano, where virtually every player on every contending team had some pro experience. The days of raw rookies and part-time, hockey-playing amateurs were now truly over, though participating Canadians were hardly well paid. For the 1987-88 season, Team Canada members earned $12,000 and had to pay their own living expenses. Clearly, this was a labour of love and no one was going to get rich playing for the Olympics.

The Olympics and the Pros

Heading the list of Canada's pros was goaltender Andy Moog. A member of the Edmonton Oilers from 1980 to 1987, Moog was a three-time Stanley Cup winner in 1984, 1985, and 1987, but he was now idle because of a contract dispute with Edmonton. Here was a proven, bona fide NHLer who was now allowed to play in the Olympics. Joining him, under more pleasant circumstances, was

Oilers teammate Randy Gregg. Gregg originally played for Canada at the 1980 Games as an amateur. He was taking the 1987–88 season off to pursue his dream of an Olympic medal, one which had eluded him when his team finished a disappointing sixth at Lake Placid. Gregg planned to rejoin the Oilers after the Olympics.

Many of Gregg's and Moog's teammates were either to embark on a pro career as soon as the Olympics were over or already had pro experience and wanted the chance to represent Canada internationally. Tim Watters, another 1980 Olympian, was loaned at the last minute to the team by the Winnipeg Jets for whom he was playing; Ken Berry, another '80 alumnus, used the opportunity as a springboard to sign with Vancouver; Jim Peplinski and Brian Bradley were loaned to the team by the home town Calgary Flames (Paul Reinhart was also slated to join the team, but a back problem prevented his participation); Steve Tambellini was loaned by the Canucks and Ken Yaremchuk by the Leafs; Bob Joyce would join Boston and Trent Yawney Chicago right after the Games. And, at the other end of the spectrum, amateur Chris Felix had spent the last three years with the Olympic team, time that helped him mature as a player and persuaded Washington to take enough of an interest in him to sign him after the Olympics had ended.

Canada's "Other" Canadians

Because pros were now allowed to compete, and dual-citizenship laws were increasingly open in this evermore global village, there were many Canadian-born players on other hockey teams as well. In fact, three countries—Norway, Austria, and West Germany—could boast of having a starting goalie who was born and raised in Canada—Vernon Mott (Norway), Brian Stankiewicz (Austria), and Karl Friesen (West Germany). In all, 21 Canadians were playing for other countries in the Olympic hockey tournament, most of them having played pro in smaller European centres for a number of years, not good enough for the NHL any longer, but not willing to abandon their Olympic dream, either.

Randy Gregg's Olympic sweater.

1988, Calgary, Alberta

1992

Albertville, France

February 8–23, 1992

GOLD	Unified Team
Silver	CANADA
Bronze	Czechoslovakia
Fourth	United States
Fifth	Sweden
Sixth	Germany
Seventh	Finland
Eighth	France
Ninth	Norway
Tenth	Switzerland
Eleventh	Poland
Twelfth	Italy

TEAM CANADA

Sean Burke, Trevor Kidd, Kevin Dahl, Curt Giles, Gord Hynes, Adrien Plavsic, Dan Ratushny, Brad Schlegel (*captain*), Brian Tutt, Jason Woolley, Dave Archibald, Todd Brost, Dave Hannan, Fabian Joseph, Joe Juneau, Patrick Lebeau, Chris Lindberg, Eric Lindros, Kent Manderville, Wally Schreiber, Randy Smith, Dave Tippett, Sam St. Laurent (*did not play*), Dave King (*coach and general manager*), Terry Crisp (*assistant coach*), Wayne Fleming (*assistant coach*)

Team Canada's Hockey Season

As had become customary, Team Canada had been in training for the Olympics since August of the previous year, though the small crew of 18 players who showed up for the first day of camp, which included seven members from the 1988 Calgary Games, certainly did not even faintly resemble the final roster on opening night in Albertville six months later. In fact, of the returnees, only Sean Burke and Jason Woolley actually played in both Olympics. Of prime concern was the team's training centre in Alberta. Because the altitude at Albertville would be 500 metres higher, conditioning became a priority. Also, this would be Dave King's third trip to the Games with Canada; still medal-less, he, too, had something to prove this trip.

Canada's Small Towns

In the four years between Olympics, Canada's National Team played many exhibition games against varying levels of competition, mostly in small Canadian cities that didn't often get the chance to see such quality of hockey. The team's itinerary included stops in Kapuskasing, New Liskeard, Iroquois Falls, and Elliot Lake in Northern Ontario, the remote Powell River in British Columbia, Maniwaki, Quebec, and Sherwood Park, and Red Deer in Alberta.

Perhaps most cherished of all was Canada's game against a Russian team in White Court, Alberta, where a local women's hockey team, the Hot Paddies, put up a $28,000 guarantee to bring the game there on

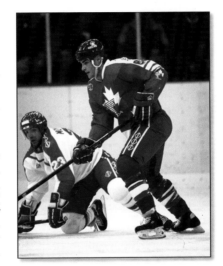

Eric Lindros had five goals and eleven points for Canada in 1992.

January 1, 1992. Another gem of a game took place in Barrs Head, Alberta in a rink that could seat only 850 people. When the Olympians visited, 1,400 people paid between $25-$50 for once-in-a-lifetime seats. Fans in these remote cities were as encouraging in their telegrams and faxes as were those in the big cities, and all players appreciated and recalled the support with great affection. Over the decades, small-town Canada had provided the NHL and Olympic teams with as many great players as had the country's metropolises; these games were not token symbols or publicity stunts but well-chosen ways of saying thanks to all the families in all the small places for making Canada the great hockey powerhouse it was.

The Pros are Here

The 1988 Games had been a watershed event in officially allowing professionals to participate in the Olympics. Four years later, all teams were recruiting their country's pros with single-minded determination. The Swedes were perhaps the most successful in their efforts and thus became the early favourites to win gold. On their blue line was Borje Salming, the 16-year Toronto Maple Leafs veteran. He was joined by Hakan Loob, Tommy Soderstrom, Mats Naslund, and Bengt Gustafsson, all seasoned NHLers. The Finns also fielded a pro-preference team that included Kari Eloranta, Simo Saarinen, Hannu Virta, Ville Siren, Hannu Jarvenpaa, Raimo Sumanen, Petri Skriko, and Teemu Selanne. Money was also playing an ever-increasing role in the Olympics. The Czechs were all guaranteed a new Skoda car if they brought home a medal, while the Russians were even more blunt about awarding their hockey players' success: a gold was worth $3,000 a player, silver $2,000, and bronze $1,000.

Canada's Roster—A Summary

Putting together the team for the 1992 Olympics began the day after the '88 Games concluded, and Canada's entry in Albertville reflected the singular methods of hockey in Canada. Captain Brad Schlegel started with Dave King in the fall of 1988 when Olympic on-ice preparations began in earnest. Todd Brost joined the team the next fall, and in 1990 Gord Hynes, Dave Archibald, Chris Lindberg, and

Goalie Sean Burke played in seven of Canada's eight games in Albertville.

Randy Smith began their tour of duty. This, then, was the core of the 1992 team. At the same time, King was adding and scratching names from the lineup right up until days before the Games were set to begin.

The quality of the team had increased a little bit each year since Canada re-entered the Olympics in 1980, but the set-up still was nowhere near ideal. Having all amateurs would have been perfect from the point of view of preparation, but not if optimum results were being asked for. All top-notch pros would have been the route to go to maximize results, but that still was not feasible without a comprehensive agreement with the NHL, and that was not going to happen until the Americans decided the effort would be worth it.

Jason Woolley's Olympic sweater.

1992, Albertville, France

1994 LILLEHAMMER, NORWAY
February 13–27, 1994

GOLD	Sweden
Silver	CANADA
Bronze	Finland
Fourth	Russia
Fifth	Czech Republic
Sixth	Slovakia
Seventh	Germany
Eighth	United States
Ninth	Italy
Tenth	France
Eleventh	Norway
Twelfth	Austria

TEAM CANADA

Corey Hirsch, Mark Astley, Adrian Aucoin, David Harlock, Ken Lovsin, Derek Mayer, Brad Schlegel, Chris Therien, Brad Werenka, Greg Johnson, Petr Nedved, Greg Parks, Todd Warriner, Fabian Joseph, Paul Kariya, Jean-Yves Roy, Wally Schreiber, Todd Hlushko, Chris Kontos, Dwayne Norris, Brian Savage, Manny Legace (*did not play*), Alain Roy (*did not play*), Tom Renney (*coach*), Danny Dube (*associate coach*)

Build-up to the Games

The Canadian team began training in September 1993 and played perhaps their most ambitious series of tournaments and exhibition games in preparation for Lillehammer. Canada won a silver medal at the Telehockey Cup in Norway and again at the Nova Scotia International Cup. The team also played in the Globen Cup in Sweden, Deutschland Cup in Germany, and the Izvestia tournament in Moscow.

Coach Tom Renney.

They played a nine-game series against Russia, a four-game series with the American Olympians, and a series of matches against other Olympics-bound hockey nations such as the Czech Republic, Sweden, and Finland.

The Canadian Roster

Team Canada's Lillehammer line-up was again an interesting blend of NHLers and NHL-aspirants, but perhaps the most notable absentee from the squad was Toronto Maple Leaf forward Glenn Anderson. Anderson signed with the Leafs for the 1993–94 season with a guarantee from GM Cliff Fletcher that he would make Anderson available to the national team at the appropriate time. Fletcher was only too happy to oblige, but, as it turned out, the NHL rules stated that if Anderson were to leave the Leafs to play in the Olympics, he would have to clear waivers.

Obviously, he would have been claimed by some team had Toronto put him on the open market, so the Leafs petitioned NHL Commissioner Gary Bettman asking to receive special exemption for Anderson, seeing that his being put on waivers was not to get rid of him from the Leafs but to allow him to participate in the Games. Bettman, however, declined to help Anderson in his Olympic cause.

Another controversy, one that ended more positively, involved Czech-born Canadian Petr Nedved. Nedved became a Canadian citizen in July 1993 after spending three years in the Vancouver Canucks organization, but that same summer became involved in a contract dispute that saw him walk out on the team and refuse to show up for training camp that fall. Nedved's desire was to play for Canada, but because of his citizenship change he had to sit on the sidelines until December 26, 1993 before the IIHF finally gave him clearance to play for his new country.

One genuine success story in the Canadian line-up was goalie Corey Hirsch, who wound up playing every minute of the '94 Games for Canada (only the third time since 1920 that one goalie carried the whole load). Hirsch was the star of the AHL his first year as a pro (1992-93) and was confident he could earn a spot in the 1993 training camp with the New York Rangers. Such was not the case, and before the season started he was sent by the Broadway Blueshirts to Tom Renney's Olympic team, a move Hirsch saw as a demotion, a sign of failure. But by the time the Games were in full swing, he was on cloud nine. "I wouldn't have missed this for the world," he beamed. "This is just an awesome experience, the best thing that ever happened to me. And to think I started out lukewarm about the whole idea. I just didn't get it."

His epiphany came the second day of the Games, after watching downhiller Edi Podivinsky fly down the mountain to win a bronze for Canada. "It hit me then, what I'd failed to appreciate, when I realized what a chunk of his life this guy had sacrificed to do that for Canada. I'll tell you... it's a privilege to be associated even remotely with a person like that." Hirsch, too, was an inspiration to many young Olympic hopefuls after backstopping Canada to a silver medal at Lillehammer.

The Rest of the Roster

Team Canada came back from the Izvestia tournament a sorry lot, having scored just four goals in four games. This outcome led to a series of changes similar to those of other years, when one set of players stayed with the team for a long time to bolster the line-up and try to earn a spot but was then replaced by superior players at the last minute. Although Brett Lindros was injured and couldn't

Sweden's Peter Forsberg scored the decisive goal in the gold-medal shootout.

join the team, and Glenn Anderson had been refused the opportunity to play, others were able to come in and improve, among other things, the team's offence. Petr Nedved was one such player, as were Brad Werenka from the Edmonton Oilers organization and defenceman Mark Astley from his club in Switzerland. In all, close to a dozen new faces that hadn't played at the Izvestia in December were starters in Lillehammer six weeks later.

As for the rest of the roster, virtually every Canadian on the Olympic team went on to play in the NHL: Astley joined the Buffalo Sabres, Adrian Aucoin the Canucks, David Harlock the Leafs, and Todd Hlushko signed with the Flyers right after the Games. Greg Johnson became a Red Wing, Fabian Joseph an Edmonton Oiler, and Paul Kariya emerged as a bona fide superstar in Anaheim. Chris Kontos had ten years of part-time NHL experience. Manny Legace became a Whaler in Hartford, Jason Marshall a St. Louis Blue, Derek Mayer signed with the Senators, Dwayne Norris joined Quebec, Jean-Yves Roy the Rangers, Brian Savage the Habs in Montreal, Chris Therien the Flyers, and Todd Warriner became a fine young player with the Leafs. Tom Renney, of course, moved on to become bench boss for the Canucks. All of these players gave further credence to the sound belief that Hockey Canada was doing its job, providing competition superior to any other these players could have gained in Junior or elsewhere in the world (outside the NHL), giving them an incredible national and emotional experience second to none, and providing the best training imaginable for a career in the NHL.

Shootout to Decide Gold

While this was the first time since Russia joined the Games in 1956, and Canada also participated, that the two countries did not play each other even once, the Olympics did not lack drama. What *kind* of drama was another question. After the preliminary round, the final eight teams played an elimination series of games, but because the IOC didn't want to risk sudden-death overtime going on too long, they took a page from soccer's rulebook and the Olympics featured shootouts to decide each game's winner. The resultant showdown concept was entertaining, nail-biting, and quick, but it was not popular at first among traditionalists who wanted the games to be played until a winning goal was scored, even if it meant five overtime periods to accomplish.

1998 Nagano, Japan
February 7–22, 1998

GOLD	Czech Republic
Silver	Russia
Bronze	Finland
Fourth	CANADA
Fifth	Sweden
Sixth	USA
Seventh	Belarus
Eighth	Kazakhstan
Ninth	Germany
Tenth	Slovakia
Eleventh	France
Twelfth	Italy
Thirteenth	Japan
Fourteenth	Austria

TEAM CANADA (MEN)

Patrick Roy, Scott Stevens, Chris Pronger, Eric Desjardins, Adam Foote, Rob Blake, Al MacInnis, Ray Bourque, Trevor Linden, Rob Zamuner, Steve Yzerman, Mark Recchi, Brendan Shanahan, Shayne Corson, Rod Brind'Amour, Joe Sakic, Keith Primeau, Theo Fleury, Wayne Gretzky, Eric Lindros, Joe Nieuwendyk, Martin Brodeur (*did not play*), Curtis Joseph (*did not play*), Marc Crawford (*head coach*), Andy Murray (*assistant coach*), Mike Johnston (*assistant coach*), Bobby Clarke (*general manager*)

Organizing the Organizers

Perhaps the biggest task of all facing Canada in Nagano was the proper coordination of the many groups, teams, and interests who had a hand in organizing Team Canada. Bob Nicholson, senior vice-president of the Canadian Hockey Association, selected the three men to run the on-ice show for Nagano on January 30, 1997—Bob Clarke, general manager of the Philadelphia Flyers; Bob Gainey, GM of the Dallas Stars; and, Pierre Gauthier, GM of the Ottawa Senators. Opined Nicholson: "When we did our search and interviewed various general managers, we thought it would be best to have people who are

Brendan Shanahan (left) and Wayne Gretzky get ready for a faceoff.

Wayne Gretzky and Finland's Jari Kurri compete for a loose puck.

involved in the day-to-day operations of NHL teams. In Clarke, Gainey, and Gauthier, I believe we have three of the sharpest minds in hockey… all three have impeccable credentials for the formidable, high-pressure, and exciting challenge that lies ahead."

Interestingly, the CHA was the one body in the IOC that didn't want pros to join the Olympics, as Nicholson confessed: "All of the European countries, along with the U.S., wanted NHL players involved because they really thought it would give better exposure to hockey globally. We were the odd federation out, so we went on side with it." However, in order, for the idea to reach fruition, much had to be worked out. The NHL had to plan and agree to stop play in the league for some 17 days; the NHL Players' Association had to negotiate with the league regarding the closing, supplying the players to the various competing teams, and making practical arrangements for the players' participation.

Naming the Roster

One day after being named Team Canada GM, Bob Clarke pronounced that, "there's no possible way you can have your team on August 1," thus contradicting an important piece of the negotiations that had been worked out with the IOC for NHL participation. The IOC relented and allowed Canada until December 1 to name the roster, thus giving the GM troika time to assess the performance of the players during the 1997–98 season, and giving players on the selection bubble a chance to showcase themselves and prove themselves worthy of selection.

Previous to that, some players got a chance to prove themselves at the World Championships in Helsinki in April 1997. For the sake of continuity and experience, the

three Olympic GMs had full control over the team sent to represent Canada there, with the one obvious limitation being that players on the team were on NHL clubs that didn't make the Stanley Cup playoffs. Thus, the World Championship team did not reflect at all what the GMs saw as the final Nagano roster.

Unlike selection for the 1996 World Cup, the Dream Team was chosen based on three considerations: (1) who was playing well as close to the tournament as can be judged? (2) what would be the player's role on the team? (3) who could play on a European ice surface?

The Hectic Schedule

Having Canada's best at the Olympics was something that had never happened before in hockey. Yet the logistics of participation, particularly for Nagano, was something less than ideal. Yes, the NHL closed down, but not for one hour longer than necessary. The players had only four days to practise in Calgary after the 1998 All-Star Game in Vancouver before leaving for Japan, where they played their first game just a few days later. Along the way, they had a 14-hour flight to Tokyo, a train ride into the city, and another four-hour train ride to Nagano.

The First NHL Olympics

Nagano was a test case for NHL hockey at the Olympics, a prelude to 2002 when the sport and its players would receive greater attention in a North American city in a time zone more palatable to Canadian fans. Nonetheless, the disappointments outweighed the glory in Japan. Team USA sullied its own reputation when a small number of its players trashed their rooms. Canada played well but lost a semi-final game against the Czechs in a shootout. And the Czechs and Russians played a dull gold-medal game won by the Czechs 1-0 to claim their first Olympic gold in hockey.

Canada then compounded its misery by losing to the Finns 3-2 in the bronze-medal game, and instead of coming home with an expected gold the players came home empty-handed altogether. Clarke was criticized for selecting Rob Zamuner to the team and for insulting Wayne Gretzky by making his own player, Eric Lindros of Philadelphia, team captain. Coach Marc Crawford was criticized even more roundly for not selecting Gretzky, the NHL's all-time leading goal scorer, as one of the shooters in the five-man penalty-shot showdown against Dominik Hasek. And the team was criticized for not being able to score more than once in 70 minutes of hockey against the Czechs to avoid the shootout.

In short, this was a learning experience for Hockey Canada, and out of that came an historic gold four years later.

GOLD	USA
Silver	Canada
Bronze	Finland
Fourth	China
Fifth	Sweden
Sixth	Japan

TEAM CANADA (WOMEN)

Lesley Reddon, Manon Rheaume, Becky Kellar, Therese Brisson, Fiona Smith, Judy Diduck, Cassie Campbell, Geraldine Heaney, France St. Louis, Jennifer Botterill, Lori Dupuis, Kathy McCormack, Danielle Goyette, Jayne Hefford, Stacy Wilson, Nancy Drolet, Hayley Wickenheiser, Laura Schuler, Vicky Sunohara, Karen Nystrom, Shannon Miller (*head coach*), Daniele Sauvageau (*assistant coach*), Ray Bennett (*assistant coach*), Rob Cookson (*assistant coach*)

History Made

It took eight years, but finally the women were going to the Olympics! The first officially-sanctioned IIHF World Women's Championship took place in 1990 in Canada, and later World Championships proved increasingly popular among players and fans to the point that the IOC decided to recognize women's hockey as an official medal sport. On the downside, the 1990s saw only two countries dominate—Canada and USA. On the positive side, women's hockey (both popularity and participation) in those two countries was doubling and tripling every year and in Europe the game was establishing itself firmly.

The Preparation

Because there was no women's hockey league from which to cull talent, Team Canada had to create a special season for the players. This meant inviting 28 women from across the country to live and practise together for the six months leading up to Nagano at Canadian Hockey's High Performance Centre in Calgary. During that time the women were paid a grand total of $1,854 a month and were unable to hold a full-time job because of their rigorous training schedule. Even coach Shannon Miller had to take a leave of absence from the police force in order to perform her duties for the team.

The Americans scored six goals in the third period during the round robin portion of the tournament to turn a 4-1 deficit into a 7-4 win.

The silver medal was small consolation for Team Canada's women who couldn't hide their disappointment at finishing second.

The Exhibition Season

In order to train effectively, the women had to play games, but their only true competition came from the Americans, whom they were sure to face in the finals. As a result, the two nations played each other 13 times in the weeks leading up to Nagano. The two most significant of those games came in Vancouver and Calgary in late January 1998 when 14,944 fans attended the first of those games and 15,163 came to the second game, record crowds for women's hockey games. The exhibition series saw Canada win seven and lose six, both teams scoring 37 goals apiece. The most important result, however, might have been the USA's 3-0 win in the finals of the Three Nations Cup in Lake Placid just before Christmas 1997, the widest margin of victory ever by the Americans over their northern rivals.

Tounament Format

For this inaugural Olympic appearance, the women's competition featured six teams in one pool playing a round-robin series, the top two teams advancing to a gold-medal game. There was never a doubt which teams would be in that final game, but the result of the gold-medal clash was very much up in the air. In the round robin, Canada and the USA dominated their opponents. The only difference in the standings came on the final day when the Americans handed Canada a substantial 7-4 loss, a prelude to the final game of the tournament for gold. What was stunning about that defeat was that the teams were tied 1-1 in the first period and after 40 minutes, and early in the third the Canadians exploded for three goals to take what looked to be an insurmountable 4-1 lead. The Americans, however, scored six goals in a row to turn the sure loss into a handy victory.

Going for Gold

In the gold medal game, both teams realized the stakes had never been higher. They came out and played a tentative first period that resulted in no goals and few good chances, but early in the second the Americans score on a power play. They score midway through the third period to take a 2-0 lead, but a late goal by Danielle Goyette gave Canada new life. With goalie Manon Rheaume on the bench, however, the Canadians could not sustain pressure in the USA end and gave up an empty-net goal to make the final score 3-1. Despite having beaten the Americans in the finals of all four previous World Championships for gold, they left Nagano in tears with a silver medal. Nonetheless, the tournament represented a breakthrough for women's hockey and created a fierce two-team rivalry that has yet to be broken.

2002 Salt Lake City, Utah

February 9-24, 2002

GOLD	CANADA
Silver	United States
Bronze	Russia
Fourth	Belarus
Fifth	Sweden
Sixth	Finland
Seventh	Czech Republic
Eighth	Germany
Ninth	Latvia
Tenth	Ukraine
Eleventh	Switzerland
Twelfth	Austria
Thirteenth	Slovakia
Fourteenth	France

TEAM CANADA (MEN)

Martin Brodeur, Curtis Joseph, Rob Blake, Eric Brewer, Adam Foote, Ed Jovanovski, Al MacInnis, Scott Niedermayer, Chris Pronger, Theo Fleury, Simon Gagne, Jarome Iginla, Paul Kariya, Mario Lemieux, Eric Lindros, Joe Nieuwendyk, Owen Nolan, Mike Peca, Joe Sakic, Brendan Shanahan, Ryan Smyth, Steve Yzerman, Ed Belfour (*did not play*), Pat Quinn (*head coach*), Ken Hitchcock (*assistant coach*), Jacques Martin (*assistant coach*)

A golden celebration caps Canada's first gold medal in 50 years.

Gretzky Takes Control

After retiring as a player in the spring of 1999, Wayne Gretzky took a year off and virtually disappeared. When he emerged, he was part owner of the Phoenix Coyotes and back in the game in a serious way. Soon after, on November 8, 2000, Canadian Hockey Association president Bob Nicholson hired Gretzky to oversee the men's team as it prepared for the 2002 Olympics. Gretzky, a member of the Edmonton Oilers in the 1980s, the highest-scoring team in NHL history, didn't hesitate to accept the position and vowed to craft a winning team. He promised to choose players based on skill over size, speed over strength, and excitement over system-based coaching. He defied critics by boasting that Canada was not only the greatest hockey nation in the world but that it was the most skilled and could play high-tempo hockey with any nation, independent of hitting and fighting and physical intimidation.

To that end, he chose former teammate Kevin Lowe as his right-hand man and Toronto Maple Leafs coach Pat Quinn as the boss for Salt Lake City. Quinn's Leafs didn't play the popular but boring trap, and Gretzky fully intended to choose a team that fit Quinn's style and vice versa.

Goalie Martin Brodeur celebrates victory with his teammates.

Salt Lake

Everything about 2002 was different from 1998 in Nagano. Gretzky's presence and attitude created a new confidence in the team, and the player selection was boosted by the un-retiring of Mario Lemieux, who had been out of the game when Japan hosted the Olympics four years earlier. Gretzky immediately named Lemieux to the team first and foremost, making him team captain and making it clear this would be a calm, experienced team. He then chose the best players in the country, declaring that if he went with the best they would have the skill to fill whatever role was asked of them (checker, penalty killer, etc.). The team held a mini-training camp prior to the start of the 2001-02 season, and this was pretty much the team that went to Utah, with one notable exception. Jarome Iginla started the NHL season off so well that Gretzky named the Flames star to the team just before Christmas.

The Preliminary Round

Once the team congregated in Salt Lake, it was Quinn's job to set the lines and make a team of this talented group of players. In his mind, the three preliminary round games were meaningless because no team was eliminated at this stage, so he saw these games as a chance to see what worked and what didn't. The first game, a bad 5-2 loss to Sweden, helped him decide on his goalies. His own Curtis Joseph of the Leafs was in net for that first game, and Quinn went with Martin Brodeur for the second game. Brodeur played better and better as the tournament progressed, and Joseph never played another minute.

Gold

Canada played Finland in the quarter-finals and won the game 2-1 thanks to goals from Joe Sakic and Steve Yzerman and great goaltending by Brodeur. Everyone the world over expected the next opponent to be Sweden, but Tre Kronor lost to Belarus 4-3 in one of the greatest upsets in international hockey history. The Canadians cruised to the finals with a 7-1 win.

The gold-medal game proved to be an all-North American finals after USA beat Russia in a thrilling 3-2 semi-finals. The last international game of significance between the two countries came at the 1996 World Cup, won late in the final game of the best-of-three by USA. Some 15 players from that team were on USA's Olympic squad for 2002 while Canada's lineup was largely revamped. Although the Americans scored the first goal of the game, Iginla and Paul Kariya scored before the first period ended to give Canada a 2-1 lead. Brian Rafalski tied the game later in the second for USA, but a Sakic goal near the end of the period gave his country a lead it never relinquished.

Canada scored two unanswered goals in the third to put an exclamation mark beside the 5-2 score, and at the final horn the Canadians leaped in the air in celebration, the first Olympic hockey gold in exactly half a century. After the medals were presented, the story of the lucky loonie emerged as Gretzky revealed the one-dollar coin which the Edmonton ice crew had buried under centre ice of the E-Center to give the Canadians luck. From that day to this, every Canadian team competing internationally has copied the good luck charm to almost perfect success.

The victory worked on many levels. First, it atoned for the disappointment of 1998. It also paved the way for Canada to focus on skill at every level of international play. It turned out to be the last great hurrah of Mario Lemieux's career (excepting the 2004 World Cup), and it saw the emergence of Iginla as not just a great player but a leader and true star. The game was watched by more than ten million Canadians and started a streak of gold medals that continued with the juniors, the women, and the men at the World Championship. Salt Lake provided the country with renewed pride and re-confirmed it as the hockey capital of the world.

GOLD	**CANADA**
Silver	United States
Bronze	Sweden
Fourth	Finland
Fifth	Russia
Sixth	Germany
Seventh	China
Eighth	Kazakhstan

TEAM CANADA (WOMEN)

Lesley Reddon, Manon Rheaume, Becky Kellar, Fiona Smith, Sami Jo Small, Kim St. Pierre, Therese Brisson, Isabelle Chartrand, Geraldine Heaney, Cheryl Pounder, Colleen Sostorics, Dana Antal, Kelly Bechard, Jennifer Botterill, Cassie Campbell, Lori Dupuis, Jayna Hefford, Danielle Goyette, Caroline Ouellette, Cherie Piper, Tammy Lee Shewchuk, Vicky Sunohara, Hayley Wickenheiser, Daniele Sauvageau (*head coach*), Melody Davidson (*assistant coach*), Wally Kozak (*assistant coach*)

The Coaching Staff

A point of pride for the women's team was having a woman coach, something that separated Canada from most other participating nations. In the case of head coach Daniele Sauvageau, the team had not just a leader but a pioneer and mentor. Sauvageau started as an assistant coach in the under-19 program in 1996 and worked her way up to assistant coach for Nagano in 1998. She became head coach of the National Team the next year and led Canada to gold at the 1999 and 2001 World Championships. In 1999-2000, she also became the first woman member to join the coaching staff of a men's junior team, the Montreal Rocket of the Quebec major league.

Assistant coach Melody Davidson led the team to gold in 2000 and had also been in the organization for years, in her case dating to 1994 as an assistant at the World Championship in Lake Placid. Wally Kozak provided experience within the staff, his career as player and executive spanning all levels of major league play going back decades.

The Revenge Factor

In a tournament with only two legitimate contenders, it's possible for revenge to be a motivating factor without the players losing focus. As of February 2002, Canada had won seven straight World Championships but lost the one

Canada's women celebrate a gold they had been waiting four years to win.

Canada's defensive play made the difference in the gold medal game.

game that meant the most—the gold medal game in 1998. Four years later, on American ice, they had the chance to exact that revenge.

This revenge was hardly routine or predictable. In fact, in the months leading up to Salt Lake, it seemed clear that the Americans had pulled further ahead from Canada and that a home gold was a virtual certainty. Team USA won eight consecutive games from Canada in exhibitions prior to February 2002, and perhaps it was these results that forced coach Sauvageau to shake up the roster as she did. She dropped Nancy Drolet, a veteran of the team, and inserted Cherie Piper, who became the youngest player on the team. If her hunch was correct, it would be a move of genius; if incorrect, it would possibly cost her her coaching career.

The Olympic Tournament

As could be expected, both teams waltzed through the games leading to the finals. In the preliminary round, in fact, Canada recorded three straight shutouts and scored 25 goals in those games. The Americans, with a goals for-against aggregate of 27-1, were almost as perfect. Both teams also won their semi-finals matches, as expected, and this forced a one-game showdown for gold.

The women's final was watched by seven million Canadians, a staggering number, and they were treated to a tense, exciting finale. Caroline Ouellette scored the only goal of the first period to give Canada a 1-0 lead, and then the team ran into penalty trouble—serious penalty trouble. The American referee, Stacey Livingston, called the Canadians for eight successive minor penalties from midway through the first to midway through the second. Unbelievably, they surrendered just one goal, early in the second period, and in between bouts of penalty killing Hayley Wickenheiser managed to give the team a 2-1 lead. The back-breaking goal was scored by Jayne Hefford with just one second remaining in the second period, and as Canada went to the dressing room they were leading 3-1 with only 20 minutes separating them from a gold medal.

In the third, Canada again killed off three more penalties, allowing a goal on the last at 16:04. Now 3-2 with under four minutes to play, the Americans pressed for the tieing goal but goalie Kim St. Pierre kept them off the scoresheet. Canada had won its Olympic gold that it felt it should have won in 1998, and the victory came thanks to the finest penalty-killing effort in the history of women's hockey.

Gold	Sweden
Silver	Finland
Bronze	Czech Republic
Fourth	Russia
Fifth	Slovakia
Sixth	Switzerland
Seventh	Canada
Eighth	USA
Ninth	Kazakhstan
Tenth	Germany
Eleventh	Italy
Twelfth	Latvia

Tournament MVP   Antero Niittymaki (FIN)

Directorate Awards
Best Goalie   Antero Niittymaki (FIN)
Best Defenceman   Kenny Jonsson (SWE)
Best Forward   Teemu Selanne (FIN)

Media All-Star Team
Goal   Antero Niittymaki (FIN)
Defence   Nicklas Lidstrom (SWE), Kimmo Timonen (FIN)
Forward   Teemu Selanne (FIN), Saku Koivu (FIN), Alexander Ovechkin (RUS)

Final Standings

Group A	GP	W	L	T	GF	GA	P
Finland	5	5	0	0	19	2	10
Switzerland	5	2	1	2	10	12	6
Canada	5	3	2	0	15	9	6
Czech Republic	5	2	3	0	14	12	4
Germany	5	0	3	2	7	16	2
Italy	5	0	3	2	9	23	2

Group B	GP	W	L	T	GF	GA	P
Slovakia	5	5	0	0	18	8	10
Russia	5	4	1	0	23	11	8
Sweden	5	3	2	0	15	12	6
USA	5	1	3	1	13	13	3
Kazakhstan	5	1	4	0	9	16	2
Latvia	5	0	4	1	11	29	1

Group A

February 15	Canada 7	Italy 2
	Finland 5	Switzerland 0
	Czech Republic 4	Germany 1
February 16	Canada 5	Germany 1
	Finland 6	Italy 0
	Switzerland 3	Czech Republic 2
February 18	Switzerland 2	Canada 0
	Germany 3	Italy 3
	Finland 4	Czech Republic 2
February 19	Finland 2	Canada 0
	Germany 2	Switzerland 2
	Czech Republic 4	Italy 1
February 21	Canada 3	Czech Republic 2
	Switzerland 3	Italy 3
	Finland 2	Germany 0

Group B

February 15	Sweden 7	Kazakhstan 2
	Slovakia 5	Russia 3
	Latvia 3	USA 3
February 16	Russia 5	Sweden 0
	Slovakia 6	Latvia 3
	USA 4	Kazakhstan 1
February 18	Russia 1	Kazakhstan 0
	Sweden 6	Latvia 1
	Slovakia 2	USA 1
February 19	Russia 9	Latvia 2
	Slovakia 2	Kazakhstan 1
	Sweden 2	USA 1
February 21	Kazakhstan 5	Latvia 2
	Slovakia 3	Sweden 0
	Russia 5	USA 4

Playoffs

Quarter-finals

February 22	Russia 2	Canada 0
	Sweden 6	Switzerland 2
	Finland 4	USA 3
	Czech Republic 3	Slovakia 1

Semi-finals

February 24	Finland 4	Russia 0
	Sweden 7	Czech Republic 2

Bronze Medal Game

February 25	Czech Republic 3	Russia 0

Gold Medal Game

February 26	Sweden 3	Finland 2

GOLD	Canada
Silver	Sweden
Bronze	USA
Fourth	Finland
Fifth	Germany
Sixth	Russia
Seventh	Switzerland
Eighth	Italy

Tournament MVP
Hayley Wickenheiser (CAN)

Directorate Awards
Best Goalie   Kim Martin (SWE)
Best Defenceman   Angela Ruggiero (USA)
Best Forward   Hayley Wickenheiser (CAN)

All-Star Team
Goal   Kim Martin (SWE)
Defence   Carla MacLeod (CAN),
     Angela Ruggiero (USA)
Forward   Hayley Wickenheiser (CAN),
Gillian Apps (CAN), Maria Rooth (SWE)

Group A	GP	W	L	T	GF	GA	P
Canada	3	3	0	0	36	1	6
Sweden	3	2	0	1	15	9	4
Russia	3	1	0	2	6	16	2
Italy	3	0	0	3	1	32	0

February 11	Canada 16	Italy 0
	Sweden 3	Russia 1
February 12	Canada 12	Russia 0
February 13	Sweden 11	Italy 0
February 14	Canada 8	Sweden 1
	Russia 5	Italy 1

Group B	GP	W	L	T	GF	GA	P
USA	3	3	0	0	18	3	6
Finland	3	2	0	1	10	7	4
Germany	3	1	0	2	2	9	2
Switzerland	3	0	0	3	1	12	0

February 11	Finland 3	Germany 0
	USA 6	Switzerland 0
February 12	USA 5	Germany 0
February 13	Finland 4	Switzerland 0
February 14	Germany 2	Switzerland 1
	USA 7	Finland 3

Placement Games

February 17	Russia 6	Switzerland 2
	Germany 5	Italy 2

Seventh Place Game

February 20	Switzerland 11	Italy 0

Fifth Place Game

February 20	Germany 1	Russia 0 (OT/SO)

Playoffs
Semi-finals

February 17	Canada 6	Finland 0
	Sweden 3	USA 2 (OT/SO)

Bronze Medal Game

February 20	USA 4	Finland 0

Gold Medal Game

February 20	Canada 4	Sweden 1

Men

#	Pos	Name	GP	G	A	P	Pim
39	F	Brad Richards	6	2	2	4	6
15	F	Dany Heatley	6	2	1	3	8
12	F	Jarome Iginla	6	2	1	3	4
9	F	Shane Doan	6	2	1	3	2
26	F	Martin St. Louis	6	2	1	3	0
44	D	Chris Pronger	6	1	2	3	16
21	F	Simon Gagne	6	1	2	3	6
91	F	Joe Sakic	6	1	2	3	0
97	F	Joe Thornton	6	1	2	3	0
40	F	Vincent Lecavalier	6	0	3	3	16
14	F	Todd Bertuzzi	6	0	3	3	6
6	D	Wade Redden	6	1	0	1	0
61	F	Rick Nash	6	0	1	1	10
52	D	Adam Foote	6	0	1	1	6
94	F	Ryan Smyth	6	0	1	1	4
4	D	Rob Blake	6	0	1	1	2
28	D	Robyn Regehr	6	0	1	1	2
24	D	Bryan McCabe	6	0	0	0	18
3	D	Jay Bouwmeester	6	0	0	0	0
33	F	Kris Draper	6	0	0	0	0
30	G	Martin Brodeur	4	0	0	0	0
1	G	Roberto Luongo	2	0	0	0	0

In Goal	GP	W-L-T	Mins	GA	SO	GAA
Martin Brodeur	4	2-2-0	238:40	8	0	2.01
Roberto Luongo	2	1-1-0	118:58	3	0	1.51

Women

#	Pos	Name	GP	G	A	P	Pim
22	F	Hayley Wickenheiser	5	5	12	17	6
7	F	Cherie Piper	5	7	8	15	0
10	F	Gillian Apps	5	7	7	14	14
13	F	Caroline Ouellette	5	5	4	9	4
16	F	Jayna Hefford	5	3	4	7	0
17	F	Jennifer Botterill	5	1	6	7	4
15	F	Danielle Goyette	5	4	2	6	6
26	F	Sarah Vaillancourt	5	2	4	6	2
8	F	Katie Weatherston	5	4	1	5	2
77	F	Cassie Campbell	5	0	5	5	2
2	F	Meghan Agosta	5	3	1	4	2
11	D	Cheryl Pounder	5	2	2	4	6
3	D	Carla MacLeod	5	2	2	4	2
61	F	Vicky Sunohara	5	1	2	3	2
27	F	Gina Kingsbury	5	0	3	3	2
5	D	Colleen Sostorics	5	0	1	1	6
4	D	Becky Kellar	5	0	1	1	2
9	D	Gillian Ferrari	5	0	0	0	0
32	G	Charline Labonte	3	0	0	0	0
33	G	Kim St. Pierre	2	0	0	0	0

In Goal	GP	W-L-T	Mins	GA	SO	GAA
Charline Labonte	3	3-0-0	180:00	1	2	0.33
Kim St. Pierre	2	2-0-0	120:00	1	1	0.50